Potpourri: A Collection of Literary Works

To Aunt Bobby
I'm so glad God brought
us back together!

Jerlean

Columbia Writers Alliance
Columbia, South Carolina

Printed in the United States of America

2nd Printing

www.colawriters.com

ISBN 1-59872-293-X-1

Dedication Page

The Columbia Writers Alliance would like to first acknowledge God as head of our lives, and as giver of our talents and inspiration. We would also like to send a warm thank you to our family, friends, and affiliates who have supported us through this endeavor.

Writer's Prayer

Father,

In The Name of Your Son, Jesus:

We as writers Lord,
Bind our will to the Will of God.
Bind our minds to the mind of Christ.
Bind our feet to the paths we have always been ordained to walk in these days.
Bind our hands to the work we have always been ordained to do in the Kingdom of God.
Bind ourselves to the Truth of the Word with its supernatural power to heal and make whole through the gifts and talents thou has bestowed upon us.

We know full well there is nothing we can do or be without you. We are yours for this day and forevermore, Lord. We trust you to keep us and crowd us towards yourself. Thank you for your mercy and grace that you are extending to us every day.

In Jesus' Name...Amen

Table of Contents

Author **Page**

Table of Contents

Author **Page**

Table of Contents

Author **Page**

Table of Contents

Dorothy R. Carter

Poet, Aspiring Writer. Mrs. Carter is one of Columbia's newest poets. She has written over 75 poems. She is working on combining her poetry into a book of poems and collaboration with other writers to form an anthology. Mrs. Carter is married and is the proud parent of one daughter and one granddaughter. Her hobbies are writing poetry, knitting, crocheting and other creative works.

Alicia

Bright as a shining star
Fresh as a cool summer breeze
Radiant and charming as a butterfly.

Sweet as an apple
Beautiful as a jay bird
Lovely as a rose

Alicia, Alicia
All that and more!

Junk

I have a lot of junk in my trunk
I carry it around every day

I carry it to breakfast, lunch
And dinner

I lay down with it
I wake up with it

I complain about it
Pray about it
Scream about

Sometimes I sing about it

You would think I would try to get rid of it.
Butt,
I will fight you
if you try to take it away.

The Hood

If you came from the hood
You can live in Hollywood

Do not listen to anyone,
If they say you are no good

Do not let what they say
Determine your livelihood

Stand up straight with your head up high
Because you know you should

Be a good role model for your
Family and neighborhood

Don't compromise your value
You can rise to sainthood.

Forgiving

The power of forgiving is an inner peace.

Forgiving is the greatest peace
we can give ourselves.

Forgiving can give us a healing power to see
all beauty in the universe.

Forgiving changes us into positive,
thankful human beings.

Forgiving strengthens our spiritual faith.

Where I'm From

I am from black and white
from all over the world
they stood by me.

I am from black eye peas,
collard greens and corn bread
that hold me all day.

I am from that little country church
that stood on the dirt road.

I am the moon, sun
and the sky that sees everything.

I am from the air we breath which
puts life in all of God's creations.

A Good Mother

A good mother is more precious than jewels and worth more than gold. When she has God in her life she has set a firm foundation for herself and her family.

A good mother knows that she is a leader and a teacher because she knows that she is the greatest influence in her child's life.

A good mother will teach her family that the greatest thing they can do for themselves is love and respect their body. In that way they will not let anyone abuse and misuse them.

A good mother will teach her family that they have power; yes I mean power to do and become anything that they want to.

A good mother can and will make you believe that you can become a Doctor, Lawyer, Teacher, Preacher or President of this great nation.

A good mother will teach her family that if you can dream it, and believe it you will achieve it.
A good mother will teach her family that every problem has a solution, that we will have trials and tribulations and that we can see every problem as an opportunity to grow.

A good mother will teach her family to have strength and courage to stand up for what is right because she knows when you stand up for what is right you will not fall for anything.

A good mother will not let anyone separate her from the love of God. She will have enough vision to know her weaknesses. She may get perplexed, but will not despair, persecuted but not abandoned, struck down but not destroyed.

A good mother does not need the outside world to validate her self-worth because Jesus died on the cross to save us all.

A good mother is always <u>first</u> to take care of herself so that she can be A GOOD MOTHER!

Chocolate Chip

You are my chocolate chip
when I see you I get on an ego trip.

I want our friendship
to turn into a courtship.

I am mesmerized
by your goo-goo eyes.

You hypnotize me
with your lullabies.

This makes me see butterflies.

Why can't we get together to
compromise and socialize.

I Am Miss Right

I am miss right
I don’t need and I am
Not looking for a
Mr. Right

I am committed to a
Relationship with Myself

My purpose is to work
For harmonious atmosphere
For my life
YES

When I wake up in the morning
I am glad to be thinking about
What I am going to do for myself

Joy and happiness will be my centerpiece.
I deserve and will be respected

I love the feeling of freedom
I believe now I can breathe better
After I drop that 250 pound machine

Rev. Geneva D. Simpkins

Rev. Geneva D. Simpkins, a native of Camden, AL. is a strong believer in our Lord and Savior Jesus Christ. She is a faithful wife of her husband, Deacon Timothy Simpkins, and a loving mother to her daughter, Candia D. Simpkins. Rev. Simpkins and her family has lived in SC for 28 years. They are members of the Mt. Zion Missionary Baptist Church. Rev. Simpkins is an inspirational writer and the author of her first book, "Life of Holiness."

My Mother's Day Miracle

One mother's day morning; I awakened in despair,
My heart encumbered with a load of care,
I looked to my master up above,
Dear father, dear father, I need your love.

I know you don't want me to feel so much sorrow!
Lord I feel as through there's no tomorrow!!
As I talked to him everything became still,
I looked around my room,
and I thought is this real?

For even the birds at my window stopped chirping,
And off in the distance came angelica singing!
I felt the presence of angels sitting all around me,
The sorrow and pain went away
and God sent peace and I was free

There were two angels that stood by
my closet and bedroom door,
I looked at them and I saw the outline
of the beautiful golden garments they wore.

So that mother's day morning I awake in despair
But Jesus showed me just how much he cared
So whenever you feel like your heart
has been broken,
Call on Jesus; he'll be there to hear
your first words spoken.

I Got Caught Up in God's Anointing

I never stepped out to gain this world,
That was not my intention,
I never wanted to be in the spotlight,
Dear lord that was not my mission.

I didn't come forth for people to see me,
That was never in my mind,
I didn't come forth because of man,
I chose to work for God all the time.

I got caught up in God's anointing,
I came forth in God's power,
There was no idea that this was coming,
I just happened to be under his holy shower.

Yes I was inspired by other people,
I desired to know God like they did too,
But I got caught up in God's anointing.
Lord I know this anointing came from you.

Lord you said in your word in your holy book,
All who come you will in no wise cast out,
I opened my heart that day, you came in,
I know you changed me and that is no doubt.

Lord you've known my heart right from the start,
I didn't come to be seen,
But I got caught up in God's anointing,
That's how I happen to be on the scene.

Working for God that's my desire,

Calling mankind unto salvation,
Preaching your word to heal the sick,
Bringing all to justification.

I got caught up in God's anointing,
Filled with the spirit of love,
Lord I know that you are moving in my life,
You've given me the power from above.

I got caught up in God's anointing,
God's anointing is upon me,
His peace, his love, his joy forever,
Under God's anointing I desire to be.

Lord I love you with all my heart,
Your desire is my desire, your will my will,
I got caught up in God's anointing,
I'm not a fake but I'm real.

I don't shack with God, nor court him.
We have a strong relationship,
Between us there's a strong commitment,
From my heart his praise is upon my lips.

I got caught up in God's anointing,
I know what he told me to do,
I'm here because, he called me,
I'm not a fake I'm true.

Lord the devil he tries to stop me,
He tries to show me down,
But I am caught up in God’s anointing,
My feet are on solid ground.

God’s Whole Armour

A war had started in the heaven one day,
And God needed soldiers to fight,
They had to be strong and steadfast,
And always stand for what's right.

God told them I’ll fight with you,
I'll be right by your side,
I'll never leave nor forsake you,
With my children I’ll always abide.

Upon you I put my whole armor,
All bright and shiny and new ,
I know you'll wear it with honor,
I fashioned it just for you.

My son Jesus has already shed his blood,
Through belief in him you'll have your protection,
So upon your hands I place,
The helmet of salvation.

The belt of truth I tie tightly around your waist,
You must speak the truth at all times,
My soldiers must tell no lies,
For in my heavenly home liars will have no place.

I give you the breastplate of righteousness,
This piece will protect your hearts,
For you'll fighting against a vicious enemy,
And he throws his fiery darts.

In your right hand I put the shield of faith,
Every solder must have this you see,

For with faith you stand on my promises,
Because faith is very pleasing to me.

In your left hand take the sword of the spirit,
For this is my holy word,
Stand and tell it to every nation,
For my word it must be heard.

Your feet are shod for the preparation of peace,
For my soldiers seek peace and pursue it,
For your God is a God of order not chaos,
And I'm also a God of truth and spirit.

And don't forget prayer, this is my greatest weapon,
Against the enemy you see,
So always pray continuously,
For with prayer the enemy will flee.

After fitting his army with his armor,
God looked them over with pride,
Now go and fight this battle ;he told them,
And don't worry for I'm right by your side.

So God's soldiers went out into battle,
All dressed in their battle array,
And they fought and won with the victory,
Not one did the enemy slay.

Preparing for God’s Glory

This old house is not my home,
I didn't come here to stay,
I must prepare for when God comes,
He will show me the way.

Jesus has prepared a place for me to be with him,
A beautiful place with gates of pearl, and streets all paved
with gold.

I’ll see the angels oh so bright,
someday I’ll sing with them,
I'll walk with Jesus, talk with him,
his hand he'll let me hold.

But until then I must prepare by staying
right with God,
Believe his word hold on to them, and
plant them in my heart,

Sometimes this life gets very lonely, and my journey gets
real hard, But Jesus stands
right by my side, he's with me from the start.

And while I wait for my Savior
I’ll tell about his love,
His saving grace, the peace he gave,
His love from up above

To show us how to live this life,
and prepare us all for glory.

The Thief on the Right Side

I've been a thief and a robber all my life.
But this man has done no crime.
I deserve to be punished for my strife.
But this man is being punished for loving everyone
And giving them his time.

Even my friend on the other side, agrees with the crowd below.
If you are the son of God , he cried
then save your self and us

But I rebuked him saying, do you not fear God?
This man has done no wrong,
so why do you hate him so.
We deserve our punishment, but he is innocent.
He does not deserve to be tried.

I turned to the innocent man, for I
know that he is God's son
And I said this one thing before I died,

Lord remember me when you
enter into your kingdom.

And this loving man took just a second,
To look into my eyes.

I tell you the truth he said,
Today you will be with me in paradise.

My Precious Little Boy

My precious little boy
I couldn't keep you long.
But the little time you spent with me;
you brought me extra joy!!!
I couldn't bring you home so all the folks could see;
How very, very sweet you were;
my precious little Timothy.
I love you very much; I hope you know that son.
I wish you were here right now!
we'd have lots of fun.
But God had other plans for you.
up in His heavenly home.
My precious little Timothy;
all dressed in baby blue............

Washed in the Crimson Tide

As I stood beneath His Cross.
My heart went out to Him.
He poured out His blood for you and I.
That none would be lost.

There beneath the rugged cross.
My savior bled and died.
come one and all, oh don't be lost.
Be washed in the crimson tide.

Yes, there is room at the cross of Jesus.
For a billion souls to abide.
With great love He came to save us.
Oh, be washed in the Crimson Tide.

Jesus said, come ye that are weary.
I will by no means cast you aside.
come all who are thirsty.
and be washed in the Crimson Tide.

A Circle of Love

There is a special Ring I wear
that signifies a circle of Love
a never ending circle
created from above.

Its not My wedding ring
although I wear it too
this ring has a special name
a name the angels sing.

The name that's on this ring
is written upon my heart
engraved with flames of fire
written by the finger of God.

Jesus is the name upon this special ring
a special circle of love
of which the angels sing.

Yes, there is a special Ring I wear
that signifies God's love
a never ending circle
created from above.

Stephanie Suell

Stephanie Suell, pen name Virtuous, is a poet, playwright and spoken word artist. Her first book, a collection of Poetry and Short Stories, entitled "Reflections of Self' was published this year and she is currently penning her second novel entitled "This Too Shall Pass". Stephanie is an active duty Air Force member and she resides in Columbia SC with her husband and two teenage children.

To Kiss A Red Bird

My mother's stories of my father's years in the military are vivid and filled with emotional pauses. She often speaks of the months he served in Vietnam during the war and sometimes she would stop and shake her head as she reflects back. I can look in her eyes and see how painful it must have been to deal with him being so far away from home, especially during such an inopportune time.

"It was very hard for me to deal with," she would often say with a frown.

Newly married with a small child, she would spend a lot of time alone, waiting for a letter or a call from my father. She would always say that her faith in God helped her to stay strong.

"Your father's letters were a joy to receive and they came with good news."

She smiles as she recalls the days that she would sit and wait on the mailman to bring her a letter or package.

"The postman knew me by name and would nod or shake his head to let me know if there was any news from your father. On one occasion, I became very worried because I did not hear from your father for a while. My numerous letters received no response and the war loomed on. Many soldiers were returning home injured and maimed and some unfortunately never made it home. Throughout the day, I constantly prayed that God would keep your father safe and sound. Please just send me a sign I would say, I know your word is true, but I need you to show me that you hear me. It was a cloudy, overcast morning and I sat alone and sad in the living room, while you played on the floor. While I sat on the couch, a red bird flew on to the small balcony of the apartment where we lived. He perched upon the ledge of the porch and quickly ate some food that he had gathered. I watched in amazement because I rarely saw any red birds in the area where we lived and I continued to watch as the bird finished his meal and flew away. The very next day I received a letter in the mail from your father, not only was he doing well, but he was also scheduled to come home in a couple of weeks. I was thrilled and it was then that I realized that God must have sent that beautiful red bird to me as a sign that he heard my prayers. I feel that it was his way of showing me that he was around, listening and watching out for my well being. You see, God never leaves you or forsakes you," she continued, "since that day, any time I see a red bird, I blow a kiss and thank God for his blessings because I know that something good is about to happen to me, and sure enough it always does."

I listened to my mother's story of red birds for several years until I truly realized the valuable lesson that she learned from that experience. Today, I also blow kisses at red birds because they remind me of God's presence. God sends signs of his existence, but sometimes we miss them because we are too busy in the gloomy areas of our lives. Many days, we are too depressed or frustrated with life to stop and smell the roses. It is best to be patient and attentive, take a moment and wait on God because he will definitely show up on time. Too often, a simple call from a friend or a card from a loved one is our sign, but if we are not truly connected to God, we will miss the beautiful things around us and start to focus on the negative. Remember that sometimes the simple things are God's ways of showing us that he is around and constantly working on our behalf. I challenge you to take the time to smell the roses, stay connected with God and do not miss your red bird when it shows up. Be blessed…

Precious Jewels

She is wonderful.
The twinkle of my eye, the diamond that shines
through my darkness and fears, a priceless adornment
on my life.

He is charming.
An extricate design of tapestry and talent, a pearl of
exquisite taste, a symbol of royalty.

They are beautiful.
And I am proud to call them mine.

My diamond and my pearl, continuously enriching my
world, a blessing from above.

Anointing my world with their presence,
a token of God's love.

Virtuous Woman

I am woman, my worth? Above rubies and pearls
My soul has been blessed with desire
For I speak my mind with wisdom, my words are filled with power and my tongue seeks only to inspire.

Let all men rise to praise me, my children call me blessed as they seek to acquire my strength
Generations of kings and queens have I birthed and girded with righteousness
I clothe myself with strength and honor is my shield

I sing praises to my God every day
Peace, prosperity,
health I profess,
walk in faith every step of the way

Anointed, talented, divine of the Lord
No obstacles, no barriers, no stress
I walk with the aura of the queen that I am
People see me and they say, "She is blessed!"

My beauty is more than a skin-deep façade
My intelligence, you cannot comprehend
For I walk with authority, undeniable truth and ability to lead all men.
A descendant of Eve, yet a woman of rights

Proclaiming my place on the throne
Seek me,
   hear me, and take heed of my thoughts
Self reliant, almighty and strong.
Crowned with a sense of unshakable pride
I soar from the mountains on high
No power on earth can stop my flight, on the wings of eagles, I fly!
I am woman, my worth? Above rubies and pearls
My soul has been blessed from on high
I stand with an army of angels at my side
For a Virtuous woman am I

Private Room

Inviting you to join me
In my room without a view
Where imaginations are free to soar,
While conversations are few
Eliciting forbidden thoughts
Emotions spilled forth on lines
Words holding secrets
That secrete from the mind
Open pages inclined to reveal
Your hidden desires
Wants
Needs
Fantasies
Greeds
Witness…
Nuptials of pen and paper
Rhythm to rhyme
Sending your mind
On tasteful trips
Wet like damp morning dew
Deliciously sweet
Like honey kissed lips
Erotic
Poetic orgasms
No need to RSVP
Just bring an empty soul and heart
Prepare to become one with thee
Feasting on lyrical honey
For eternity

Kyra Baker

Poet, Spoken Word Artist. Kyra Baker started writing about seven years ago when she was deployed to the desert. A friend encouraged her to look around while she was there and tell him what she saw through her eyes. Her first poem, entitled, "Through Your Eyes" was the beginning of many to come. She has been encouraged along the way by a fellow English instructor at St. Leo and a USC professor, Dr. Kwame Dawes, who is an established author and poet. "He encourages me to write with color. That took some time to do, but I believe that I've got it now."

Shifting Sands

I am a dam
and the strain of the river
is causing a hairline fracture
in the heart of my casing.

The river
is contained by
my constructed
position but
the water is seeping
through; like a snail's pace
through the sever
of my barrier's deteriorated pose.

I am a dam built from
the cement of a man's hands
but slowly will I erupt
from the shifting fleet of the
waters sand.

Those Man Shoes

Zigging and zagging moving in a hip hop
craze, just a little too smooth cause you're
busy walking in those "MAN SHOES."
Yet you're jiving me saying you're at
places that you never be. Out chasing skirts,
not caring who you hurt jerking with the trends,
free falling at the comedy show; thinking that I
didn't know.

Slipping in and out of other dramatic stage
shows, but little do the skirts know that I'm
only here for a spell.

I stare in your eyes because they used to
mesmerize me with those half-truths
of your perception of what I thought was
actually reality.

But then I slowly turn away so you
wouldn't see the sad look upon my face
from yet another half attempt at a fable;
that you were thinking that you snuck
pass me underneath my table.

So clever you thought was your disguise as
you continued with your fabrications and your
little white lies. Yet I understood, because once
I use to love you.

And as I stand in front of the man, I know that
you don't see me for who I am. But when I'm no longer
standing in your face you'll look back on
this season and remember the lame reasons that you
only saw me as the homely mother, but never once
The WOMAN that I am.

Hoping For A Brighter Sunrise

I've been moody and blue, and I don't
feel like combing my hair.
I've spent the last few days writing
about my melancholy ways and the two
days before that, I swear, I felt like I was
dying from my salty disposition.

I've been crying
on my dress, it's blue too
and I bought a new pair of
shoes; yet they don't seem so new.

On yesterday I watch the sunrise,
it looked a little murky and
the air was full of mist
cause I'm feeling kinda funky.

I hope that on tomorrow
to change my ways,
but today I'm just stuck on
being blue because I miss you.

Forever Running

I was running outside
it was just a slight
breeze and I;
I was hopeful
that running would
be conducive
to my anguish.

It was silent and
I could just about
hear the ache of my heart,
it was beating slower than
the pace that I was
running; and I was
nearly at a walk.

I was talking to
my shadow and even
he scurried along, he was
too busy to take
notice that I was
feeling alone.

Yet I kept talking while
I was walking and soon fear
became my only friend, like a
nightmare with no end, it
haunted me moving swiftly
through me at a faster
pace; even in my dreams.

On tomorrow I'll go
for yet another run,
my shadow and I,
anticipating that fear
will leave me; some where
on the road that I run.

Dark Places

Dark shadows fill the ranges
of infinity, a hollowness
conceals itself behind
the pigeonholes of my
despondent eyes. Nearly
lifeless, I feel stifle
as a snail passing by.

Foreign is your presence,
a blurred metaphoric image
of you materializing
before me.

My hired hands
agitation sets in,
dejected from
fondling the tips
of an unfailing pen.

Scribing adornments
used as a metaphor for
the pith contained by
an asphyxiated
quietness.

The Lincoln Bus

Last night I had a dream that
I was Miss Celie; lifelessly gazing
as Shug left me footed on a dingy
road, full of debris and dust.

And like Miss Celie, I fainted
hoping to erase the naïve realism
of the bus haven left me behind.

Then I became a fragile child
resorting to snot nose crying and
screaming out loud.

Weeping like a sniveling
fool, as if I had been left on
the first day of school.

But I realize that it wasn't
just a dream and that there
I stood at the bus stop; knowing
that the bus had already gone-by.

Begin Anew

If we can begin anew and start to love as
if we were still kids just playing
about in school, unsuspecting
heartaches of what
lies ahead would keep
us from restraining
the love and sustain
it from lying near
stagnant; closer to being dead.

We'd stay up all night
and even if we were
to have a silly little fight,
we'd both pick up the phone
dialing each others numbers
not knowing whose
dial tone got through but we'd be in love
before we could think
about doing something
foolish that would
cause us to be through.

It wouldn't be puppy love
cause though we'd be young,
we'd be old enough to know. If
we could just unlearn the

wrongs of love,
long since done, we'd already
know all the mistakes from
the mismatching mates.

Then we'd always remember
the way we loved on
our first real kiss some where
between puppy love as kids
and the one thousandth kiss
natural progression into adulthood.

You'd agree to be my mate
and we'd both harmonize
into being the other's first real date.
Holding hands and giggling
like we were old friends, creating
memories that we'd someday
share with our own kids. And
like on *Roots* together we'd
begin our family book, foreseeing
the summation of the
production of our future youth.

I'd still shake in the corner
and would even dare to taste
tomorrow with no hidden
sorrows, if we could just tear
down the walls and let
the *jones* fall down.

Free falling without
a bungee cable, with nothing
but the air to carry us and
hold us stable.

Could it truly be?
If we could just love like kids …
we could rewind and start again.

Myra Davis-Branic

Myra Davis-Branic is a native New Yorker, now residing in the beautiful city of Columbia, SC. Mrs. Davis-Branic, an aspiring writer is currently writing a short-story based on the "coming of age experiences" of a multi-cultural girl growing up in Spanish Harlem. She is married and the mother of two young boys, and is currently working at Crayton Middle School in Columbia, SC, as Supervisor of In-school Suspension. In this capacity, she is involved in behavioral modification and counseling, and additionally mentors and offers individual academic and social instruction to students.

Worth the Weight

This last year has been a trip. New Year's Eve can't get here fast enough. It seems that the only good thing that happened in the last year was that I lost 60 pounds. But while losing my weight, I did gain wisdom through a lesson. I learned that I couldn't control what was going on around me, but I could control myself and my weight. The weird thing is I thought losing this weight would be the answer to my prayers, make everything better. "Donna", I would say to myself, "If you lose this weight you will be able to..." I would fill in the blank to fit my mood. You see, I learned how to lose weight and even keep it off, but I never learned how to deal with the people around me while I was losing weight. Early last year, my live-in boyfriend Curtis befriended two women from his job, Tasha and Alicia. They were both married, so I really wasn't threatened by the friendship.

I met Tasha first. She invited Curtis and me to a party where I met her husband and sister Faye. I felt Tasha sizing me up when I got there and felt a little self conscience, not because of my weight, because they were as big as me. I was feeling more of a "what's he doing with her?" type of vibe. Or it could have been that Curtis had earlier criticized me for over-dressing. He liked to say in public, "My girl thinks she's a plus size model." I just liked nice things. The party turned out nice and I had thought that I had met a nice friend in the end. "I like Donna; you have to bring her back."

I met Alicia and her husband when Curtis invited her to our house for a Ground Hog's Day party we threw. The theme was "bring your shadow". There was something about this Alicia that wasn't right. I couldn't put my finger on it at the time. Maybe it was the fact that she kept running to my door every time the doorbell rang, like she was expecting someone. Maybe it was how she took my rice that I steamed and asked for sugar, milk and butter to make some sort of cereal, with all of this food that I made to eat. I just thought it was rude, and even Curtis's cousin asked "Why must she have that? No one else is having that." What ever it was, she rubbed me the wrong way. When Alicia and her husband left, Tasha went on and on about how Alicia always tries to take over and how she pushes herself on people at work. Curtis acted like Alicia was one of the guys. I mentioned to Curtis that I didn't care for her and he told me that I was being silly. I backed off. I concentrated on my weight loss goals and before I knew it, I was a noticeable 25 pounds lighter. I picked Curtis up from work one day and Tasha said "Wow you really look good, now you look like the picture that Curtis has on his desk". Curtis had a picture of me that I took four years and 50 pounds ago, but I still thought it was a catty thing for her to say, I smiled it off. Alicia spoke, but she stayed in her office.

Any other time when I would call Curtis at work, she would always seem to be in his office. When we got home, I asked Curtis what if anything was said about me when his friends met me in person after seeing that picture of me in his office. He claimed nothing was said. As I continued to lose weight, only my wardrobe changed, not my insecurities. It seemed like Curtis was not as supportive as I thought he'd be. He never said anything about my weight loss and started volunteering more and more to do overtime at work. By Valentine's Day, I thought things were getting better. Curtis bought me a velour lounge outfit from Century 21 that I loved. Two months later the drama began. First, Curtis said everyone from the job was getting together to take Alicia out to cheer her up. Her husband, who was in the army, was being deployed to Iraq. I later found out that everyone had brought their partner's with them but Curtis.

Curtis was annoyed after I cross examined him, but his defense was "you go out with people from your job and I don't come." But no one from my job brought their partners. Then while cleaning our bedroom, I found a receipt from Century 21. It had my loungewear on it, but it also had lingerie-$9.99 below my $39.99 outfit. My heart started pounding and my stomach was in knots. Immediately, felt the tears welling up in my eyes.

When Curtis got home, I ambushed him. I knew intuitively that this lingerie was for Alicia. I didn't tell him that, I just kept asking, "who did you buy lingerie for?" He just kept lying and denying "I didn't buy anything, it was a mistake!" My boyfriend knows when he is overcharged.50 cents at Key Foods, but he would overlook 9.99? He bought the lingerie. Like a lot of crafty people do, he turned the tables on me, "You don't trust me." or " You're always accusing me." and of course "You're crazy!" I was never convi- nced but I let it go. "Maybe he didn't buy it" I tried to tell myself and I went on with my goals. But like wiser older women used to say, what goes on in the dark will come to light. The truth started to reveal itself. I recalled that Curtis did overtime on the day after Valentine's Day. He came home three hours later than usual and was immediately defensive when I asked him why he didn't call. That was my first clue. By July, I was down 40 pounds. I felt good about my weight loss, but not about my relationship.

Tasha and her husband invited us to their home for the Fourth of July weekend. Tasha and I sat up all night drinking and talking about how much she hated Alicia, but had to hide it because Alicia was her supervisor. After several drinks, Tasha told me that she felt Alicia and Curtis were too close and that it didn't look right. Thinking I could share, I started telling Tasha about the lingerie receipt and all the other strange things going on since Alicia started working there. Then Tasha told me how she felt her own husband had cheated and how she was almost out of the door. She shared and I shared some more, forgetting all about what my mother taught me. My mother always said, "it's o.k. to have secrets... in other words don't tell all of your business".

By the next morning, Tasha and I had not discussed what we spoke about the night before. Monday came and when I got home from work, Curtis was sitting on my leather sectional with the meanest look he could have. "What's wrong with you?" I asked. "You know what the hell you did, what you do?, get drunk and tell all my business? You told Tasha everything, you told all our business, about counseling, everything!" Whoa, I know good and damn well Tasha didn't tell him this at work.

Well, it was worse than that. I had tried to call Tasha the whole night leaving message after message for her to call me. Curtis kept saying, "don't try to call and find out who told me, you talk too much, that's it". I had to find out from Tasha what her motivation was for telling my man what we discussed. By 5:00 a.m. Tuesday, Tasha had finally picked up the phone. I guess she was too sleepy to check the caller I.D. "Hello?" "Yeah, Tasha, wake up, what's up with you telling Curtis what we talked about, I confided in you". "I'm sorry, I wasn't going to avoid you forever, I just felt really bad, I wanted everyone to get along so I told Alicia why you didn't like her and that you felt she was messing around with Curtis." "What?, you said you couldn't stand her, you are full of it." "No I meant that I don't like some of her ways, but she's o.k., You either lover her or hate her, she's a little hard to take." " That's neither here nor there Tasha. Alicia told Curtis verbatim everything I told you, but did you tell her what you said about her?" Tasha was quiet, but finally said, "I might as well tell you, because you hate me." "Damn right," I said. "Curtis will hate me too. He did buy Alicia lingerie. She showed it to me...and they were messing around, not anymore, but they were". By now I wanted to kill someone or kill an entire cheese cake. " I know how you feel," she said, "I've gone through it". "Shut up! you were sitting there playing double agent and I was stupid enough to fall for it." "I'm sorry Donna, I just wanted everyone to get along." I hung up on her. By now it was 5:45 in the morning and Curtis had to be to work at 5:30. I called his job and let him know what I knew and that I knew why he didn't want me to find out who told him. For the first time in our relationship, I stood up to him. I screamed on him and for the first time in our five year relationship, I felt powerful. I had the confidence that the weight loss alone didn't give me, but I wasn't done. I had to let every- one know not to cross Donna. The only thing Curtis asked was "what are you going to do? are you going to leave me?" I did something straight out of the movies.

You would think that after (9/ll) September 11, it would take an act of congress to get information on a deployed soldier. I was wrong. I called the army base and gave the soldier's first and last name and that of the spouse. Within 30 seconds, the army official on the other end was telling me where I could write Alicia's husband in Iraq. "Amazing", I thought. Yes I wrote Clarence, Alicia's husband, in Iraq and informed him that his wife was sleeping with my man. Next, I called Tasha's in-laws and told her very religious, scripture quoting mother in-law how Tasha really felt about her. It got ugly. By the time I was done, I no longer had the urge to kill an innocent cheese cake, I felt lighter. Curtis was walking on eggshells when he got home. I told him that it was time for me to lose more weight and I instantly lost 260 pounds when I told him to leave. I started to weaken, but I held my ground. By Thanksgiving I had lost another 20 pounds, a total of 60 pounds (not including Curtis's 260). By now I was starting to feel great about myself. At times I looked back over the past year and become a little depressed, but then I would snap myself out of it. I know it wasn't cool to tell Clarence about his wife while he was in Iraq, but she left me no choice and in end, I don't regret a thing. So now it's December 30th and I am so ready for this new year to come in. I don't mind bringing it in all by myself. Maybe I'll cook a pot of greens and some hoppin' john for luck. Maybe I'll watch the ball drop on T.V. with a glass of wine. Any way I do it, I'll just be glad this year is gone and my new year and my new life as a single, confident woman with infinite possibilities and lots to offer is less than 48 hours away, and I can't wait.

The End

How To Get The Kids To Listen

How to get the kids to listen
is not the title of a how-to book
How to get the boys to listen
(and know they shouldn't die)
over a stepped on sneaker
or a mistook look?

How to get the girls to listen
and appreciate their value or their worth
(and that it's o.k. to say no to boys)
because fifteen's too young to give birth.

How to get the kids to listen
about spirituality and making good grades
When daily the media says they have a grim future
because of gang violence and the threat of AIDS?

How to get the kids to listen
about becoming successful and giving back
When a sixteen year old tells you
"You got some nerve lady,
the only thing your generation left us was crack!"

How to get the kids to listen
that you can ease life's problems with prayer
that you can go to church for fellowship
not only when coffins and hearses are there.

How to get the kids to listen
that during reconstruction freed slaves turned
politicians and took a stand?

That we are responsible for our own actions
and cannot continue blaming the white man.

How to get the kids to listen
that a good education is the answer?
That teachers teach for love, not pay
with the hope that one young mind they mold
holds the cure for cancer.

I wish I could get these kids to listen
that their young lives have just begun, and
that they should learn from my mistakes
Lessons are better learned when you're young.

Jerlean S. Noble

Author, Poet. "Big Mama and Me" (2002). Aspiring poet (acknowledged as one of eight emerging poets in the State of SC, Nov. 2003)President & Founder of Columbia Writer's Alliance, Educated in Boston, MA and SC, wife and mother of one son. Ms. Noble is a graphic designer, manuscript secretary and coordinator of School Psychology Testing materials at USC.

Dawning Peace

So awesome thy presence Oh God
So Holy thy universal reign
Thou speak through the folds of darkest night

Commanding the dawn to open
the sun to slowly rise
shedding the cloak of twilight

Revealing panoramic brushes of gold,
  bronze and purple
Ascending the expanse of firmament

A coronation of transcendent beauty
Trailing your train of glory
The angels flutter not their wings

All is quiet in your wake

The view of David is made plain
In wonder of your majesty at Mizpah
My eyes water at the Carolina sky
Breathtaking in its splendor

There's something about
 the peace of the morning
when God opens up the day

Nanna

Pink blossoming dogwoods
 Line the walkway to "Last Mileville"
Nanna dubbed it that before she arrived.

Inside, across white marble floors, wheels spin,
 and a bell rings three times.
The sound echoes like rocks thrown against a glass pane.

Vapors mix—salves, antiseptics,
 body fluids. I peek into rooms
peppered with pot plants, vased roses,
 and pictures

Here and there, a hankie dabbed in Ode' to Pareè.
 Once these folks were generals shouting their
maternal and paternal orders.

Now, reduced to rankless has been's they are pushed

or pulled to bed—or to the grave.

Nanna sits listless, her pupils fixed on nothing
her face drawn, lips quivering as she slobbers
and drools. My eyes move to her fingers,
locked, gnarled, and knotted they lay

like dropped potatoes in her lap,
her back is tied to a metal chair
so she won't tilt—I'm told.

Nanna's long silky hair, now rice white,
I weave into two plaits. I hold
her hair and her memories, words full of wisdom,

stories of long ago dances, and kisses that made
her blush. I see them all.
With a hankie, I wipe her mouth,

push the wheelchair toward the veranda
hope the scent and the blooming dogwoods,
for just one moment, will tell her I am here.

Golden Manna

I expressed to God my hunger
I told him I could not see
The road I walked was dark and long
I was held by forces unseen
With his eyes His love consumed me
His compassion gave me strength
He commanded the waters to pour
The rain washed and made me clean
Then I received His blessings
The Word of life to succeed
For He said, "I am El-Shadi,"
And what I give you is all you need

And golden manna fell from heaven
Lighting the path for my feet to trod

Neasy

She struts, she sways
  in blush red pumps
Sporting spike stiletto heels
sexy matching underwear
hoisting twin peaks to power

His voice has caused her rain to fall
Soaking silk that sticks to skin
He makes her cry behind closed doors
He makes her moan
In front of others
Then smile at her deceit

Slowly he walks approaching her
Washing his way into her life
They share a heated private way
She closets risk
  tousled pleasure
discreet is the way …discreet

Though voices, eyes are all around
She sees and hears only him
her speech, her senses leave her
Concealed she must remain
Concealed

Neasy moves to show him all
Taking in her main desire
Screening the fire from others
That wonder about her smile

Her smile, her pout
  Raised eyebrows arch
   her movements are such
 wide-legged she sits
revealing what he already knows
Nice

Aunt Ella's Root

Come here! Set this right here and dust that right there, move this just so, do what I say gal. Yo Aunt Ella's coming up here today and I want to know if anythang's moved. I want to know when she puts something down this time—rooty old woman. She never liked me, never took to me. Ever since I married her brother, never liked me a'tall and I never done a thang to that woman. Hurry up chile, brang that broom, gitch here in that corner, make some room so that woman have plenty of space to put her stuff. Won't even drink my water, she brang her own, won't eat my food either, shoot, I'm the best cook in town. I'm not like her, I don't believe in the devil's work. I'm a Christian woman, Sunday school teacher--don't work in black magic. Rooty old woman.

Lord have mercy, every year, right at the beginning of summer the same old thing. Aunt Ella and Uncle John come up from Bamberg, SC to see my Great granddaddy, whom I called Uncle Harry. Never understood why. He just never seemed like a great granddaddy and he never complained about me calling him uncle. Anyway, they would come with a truck load of watermelon from uncle John's patch and I was always glad to see them. Following them in 2 or 3 cars was always the children—never knew just how many they had but seemed to me every time they came up there was more of them. I didn't care as long as they brought plenty of watermelon. And I didn't agree with Big Ma's claim that Aunt Ella was a witch, sounded like she said witch but she said it a little stronger maybe it was bewitch, b, ba-itch, something like that, however; she said Auntie's been putting roots or dropping roots or something. The only thing I see her drop was her tiny little butt right in the chair next to Big Ma's bed. Big Ma said that's why she can't get well. She said every time they come up she get sick until she clean her house and find the root my old auntie dropped. It's true, every time after they left I had to clean harder than I did when they came. I believe it's because one time Big Ma found a small round hard thang that looked like something between a rock and an acorn. She said that was it. We found it stuffed in the chair where aunt Ella sat and Big Ma put it in a bag and took it outside. Don't know what she did with it, don't want to know. What I do know is there was a lot of accusing Uncle Harry of having a witchy rooty sister and then a lot of praying on Big Ma's part. But Uncle Harry, he just went out and got him a shot of corn whisky and a kiss from his girl friend at the liquor house. He didn't care what Big Ma had to say then. He'd just sit, dig in the old wood stove, shuffling ashes and listening with his cigarette hanging limply out the corner of his mouth. The ashes would be so long they looked like they were almost up to the filter. No matter how much he talked, they never fell. "You always talking about my sister Cora, that ain't fair. She never done you no harm, never." Maybe she aint done me no harm Big Ma would say, but she ain't done me no good either, darn rooty old woman. That's why she so small, can't get no meat on her bone, po as she can be. If she turned sideways and stuck out her tongue, she'd look like a zipper, crazy woman. It ain't nothing but some of them roots done come back on her, that's why she look like that—real dark around the eyes and ashy around the mouth.

Funny thing. The whole time they were there, Big ma would hum and rock and watch from the corner of her eye while exchanging pleasantries. "So good to see y'all." "How's the weather down there?" "What? How many children Lester got now?" then she would end it with, "my, my, my." She would always pull me to the side and say, you keep an eye on that old woman, she's mean and contrary. No telling what she got up her sleeve. I don't want nothing from her. Then she'd say, y'all come on set down at the table, grab a bite to eat, a body ain't got no busy being hungry with all this food I got." Uncle John and the children was always ready and Aunt Ella would always roll her eyes and mouth stuff like "you just stupid." Then she'd say "Now y'all, don't y'all eat too much now, you know how upset your stomachs get and your bodies act up and stuff."

I always had to watch where I sat because if I sat too close to Big Ma, when Aunt Ella would talk like that, very sneakily telling Uncle John and that tribe of children not to eat, Big Ma would pinch me and say, see there, sneaky. Finally evening settled in and the sun was low and setting for the night. Everybody had their fill of cakes and pies and good home cooked food—that is everybody but Auntie. She always said.

"Lawdy, I ate so much this morning, just ain't got the room for anything else. John must have a cast iron stomach, eat anything."

Uncle John always fixed him 2 or 3 plates to carry back (all of which I'm sure my aunt threw out the window as soon as they were out of sight). To top everything off, Big Ma would say, "John and Ella, won't y'all just stay the night. It's sich a long ride back down that road—sich a long way to go and these poor children look like they just can't make it.." All the time knowing Aunt Ella was going to say, "No Cora, we best be gitting our way, gotta git there in time to pick the corn, git the morning crop before it gets too hot (her way of saying, not on your life woman.).

Wasn't long before we were all waving goodbye.

Everybody from Bamberg would be loaded up and waving until the cars disappeared in the distance. I do believe they had not turned the corner good before I heard Big Ma say,

> "JERLEAN git in here, get that broom, git me some hot water, lift all the pillows, that sneaky woman done hid something, I feel it in my bones. She never liked me, never took to me. Sneaky old rooty woman and I never did a thang to her."

Rain

Water free-falling from summer leaves
from so many trees sounds this morning
like walking beneath a soft waterfall.
I just want to stay here.
Allow wet pellets to kiss my face.

I wear opened toed shoes
with low soles so small puddles
wash through my toes
cross the tops of my feet
cool, refreshing.

I have a child-like giddiness
The urge to jump, to splash
Yet I must resume my adult role
and continue my jaunt to work

Such an open place, this institute
high and low buildings of Ivy League
Prestigious old and musky halls
worn carpets that stink of aged mildew

Long corridors with tiles of monotone beige
scratched from dragging nail exposed heels
All this behind the doors before me.
Dare I take the steps that lead the way
or stand still in rain
Free-falling rain

I'm engulfed by the wet smell of earth and trees
accompanied by a wind that's hardly a breeze.
From the splatter on leaves a sopping applause
of my decision to go
To return,
perhaps to more--rain.

Excerpt from Timber

Timber

The Life of Dr. Rev. John H. Smith

An old freed slave watches her son head from the sharecroppers farm to find a better life for his family. She gives him words of wisdom. Listen.

"John be real careful. Don't take no rides from no strangers. Don't go gittin in no wagons neither. You might be free as you can be right now, but trust no one. Them Patty Waggers still looking for runaways. Crazy folk, don' even care slavery's over. Must ain't heared or know nuthin bout President Lincoln or the 'mancipation proclamation." Great Grandmother Janie Smith, yelled from her wood planked porch at her oldest son as he set out to find his fame and fortune.

He'd gotten just past the end of the long dirt yard. His let his arm fall back and his hand brush the last of 4 wooden poles he and his brother'd put up for his mother's flower bed. He looked straight ahead, his mother's voice trailing his ear. It didn't bother her that he hadn't looked back. She knew he didn't believe in goodbyes. She knew she'd see him again. She also knew he was on a mission led by God His self, and if he turned his face toward her, his journey may have ended there. She continued,

"John, pay 'tension to me now. I didn't git this old being stupid. Your Pa and me taught you a lot. Now keep your hands in the Lawd's hand and everything gon' be alright for all of us." She watched her son until he was out of sight. She sat down in the old hand made wooden rocker, let her head fall back to touch the back of the chair and began to hum. The soft melodic voice, and the rhythmic squeak of the rocker blended in with the crickets and sounds of twilight. She stuck her corn pipe in her mouth and spoke softly to herself. "I'm mighty proud of my boy. Growed straight up—tall as timber" Her conversation quickly turned to a prayer.

"Lawd God, which are in heaven. You know how much we's all love you. We preciate all the Blood Yo mighty Son shed for us. You took care of us Coloreds on this plot of earth that ain't ours, but we made it. We came through. All the rapes and torture. Dem wuppins with whips and sticks, all the hangings just cause we tried to speak up or run off. Still, we trusted in You Lawd, yo Son, and the Holy Ghost and y'all brought us through. I got me 13 head of chillun, near bout worked my husband Butler to death—in the bed and on the farm. Since freedom day, we's been sharecroppin. Thanks to You. Now John's been blessed by you to find his own. You don' give him a new set of eyes and a keen mind. He ain't had no schoolin 'cept what he learned on his own. Keep him Jesus! You healed that boy and showed everybody You still a miracle worker." I don't wannna talk too much right now. My throat's clogging up with tears. I know how dirty some folks is; white and colored alike. Course, some of us coloreds just thieves. It's the only way we know how to make it. Protect John Lawd, on his way. Amen.

Louisa A. Dobbins

Improvesario. Since 1958 Louisa began her career in visual and literary arts. She has won numerous awards for her performances, including Army World Wide Best of Show Performing arts while serving in the Army in 1984.

Currently (2005) she is encouraged by the Holy Spirit to show others God's love through her involvement with her local church as well as other churches, community organizations and Disabled American Veterans. Ms. Dobbins is also an instructor of liturgical dramatics at the South Carolina extension of the Sacramento Theological Seminary and Bible College.

To Dream, To Think, To Love
(What a Lovely Precious Dream)

Oh what a lovely precious dream
That I could one day be a queen
A queen by my own right to choose
To risk a challenge, to stand to loose

To be the one who must endure
Those subtle prejudices that need a cure
But to be wise of those who can not see
Into what I dream in store for me

The pain at stake for believing a dream
Is what it takes to be a queen
The worths and values of my endeavors
Shower down in gifts from the heavens

By the maker of all God above
Who created all mortals
To dream, to think, to love

Let's Save Our Community
(In the faces of these places)

So many people are dying
 they get nothing to eat.
Some people are naked ya'll
 and sleeping in the streets.

We don' got so uppity now
 we won't pass near these streets.
The red light might stop us
 and cause us to have to speak.

We're so afraid we'll see our reflection
 in the mirror of the faces, in these places,
 which might cause us to remember
 the struggles of our dying ages

But dead is how folk see us
 through the mask we wear on our faces.

If you could see yourselves
 as your brothers and sisters do,
 impressions of achievement and prosperity
 really wouldn't mean a thing to you.
We're people united to save our community.

So remove your mask so people won't find it so
 difficult to talk to you.
Remove your mask so people won't find it so difficult
 to care for you,
Cause we're people united
Let's save our community.

A Great Man

Dr. Martin Luther King, Jr.
Was a great man of his time
And he struggled for freedom
For all mankind.

Non-violence was the robe he wore
Everyday of his life
And he had no need for arguments
Struggles nor strife

Peace was the sunshine
Every day of his life
And it shined so brightly
In times of strife

Everywhere he went he had God on his mind
Though satan would tell him
"Martin get behind,"
Still he kept God on his mind

People threatened his life
And put him in jail
But he did not worry
Because God never fails

They beat him, they scorned him
They spat on him too
But he did not worry then
Because he knew he'd come through

You see, he prayed to God to give
him the strength to endure
Because his soul was right
And his heart was pure

But one evening while he was standing all alone
God said to Martin
Son, it's time to come home

Your job may not be finished
But you ran a good race
So come home now my child
You've been blessed with my grace.

A Holy Vision
(Near Death)

There I stood beneath top soil
Quite comfortable in the place of my origin--clay.

Even in this peculiar place
  my hands are extended to
    my Heavenly Father
Behold! Just above is a hill
      where crosses bruise the earth.

Over my head, suddenly, yes suddenly
I felt wet by the moisture, the penetrating moist
  of the blood of Jesus Christ
New and whole is my soul
for I know I've been set free!
The Holy Spirit prepared my life
  to fulfill his purpose in me

I felt another flow of blood
He reminded me how He died
He anointed me with His Holy Spirit,
  again to remind me why

He said "Fulfill my great commission
  Go set my people free
Prepare them for my kingdom,
   my glory resides in thee

Tell them of my Son Jesus
   and what He's done for you
How He left His home in glory
to set all; captives free
My sheep are waiting to hear you
speak and they will follow
I will tell you what to say
and I will lead the way.
I believe the Holy Spirit as I was captive in the clay

I knew His blood had saved me
His mercy has kept me
His justice redeemed me
And His grace leads my way

Mama, They Call Me Moses

Excerpts from "My Secret Place"

I was a melancholy child. My heart was heavy and I didn't know why. I grew up near Blythewood and Killian, South Carolina.

There was a road that divided our property. It was not paved so the chain gang men kept it graded. At the base of the hill was a brook of sparkling, crystal clear water. I spent most summer evenings sitting on the bank with a 22-caliber rifle across my lap and my feet dangling in the water. The cool water felt so calm and soothing rippling through my toes and over my feet.

I kept my eyes on lookout for dangerous snakes as I listened to the rustle of the leaves and birds. I watched the squirrels and rabbits scampering about the woods at the twilight hour attempting to locate shelter before nightfall.

The various types of foliage - plant, ferns, and leaves - on the ground would exude an abundantly sweet fragrance. I kept watching the sky for the *man in the moon* "God" before mama called.

My talks with God would overwhelm me with peace and tranquillity - here in my secret place.

It was about time for me to go back to the house before the big cats came out. I may not have been able to hold off more than one even though I had the rifle.

I stayed as long as I dared when I heard "Lu-Lu, Lu-Lu time for supper!" Country people yell really loudly. " "Coming mama!" I answered in reply. "Coming mama!"

I headed back up the road barefoot and singing, "*Jesus loves me this I know for the Bible tells me so..."* Just then Bessy the cow seemed to be calling me too, " moo-moo". "I'm coming Bessy".

Oh yeah, it's time to eat. The smell of mama's cooking makes you salivate even if you're not hungry! We cleaned up and gathered around the table in our respective places, held hands, bowed our heads and mama and daddy said grace. Sometimes mama would begin speaking in tongues and prophesying! We would just look at each other while we waited on God to finish speaking through her. **AMEN**.

The food was still hot and delicious even after the long prayer. Daddy wouldn't allow us to talk or sing at the table with food in our mouths. We were a very talkative family, all except daddy and my brother Bubba, who had severe Down syndrome. So in order to be obedient to daddy's wishes, we would chew, swallow, and then talk, chew, swallow and talk. Before we left the table to wash the dishes, mama and daddy would give us our assignments.

After we finished cleaning the kitchen, we'd go to the front yard and swing, rock, and sing. Sometimes Nuety would come by with his guitar and play until he got tired. We would listen to the crickets for a while then head into the house to prepare for bed.

Mama made us pray on our knees every night. Seems like we were always praying. Mama said we were praying because of the curse.

Excerpts from: Steal Away to Jesus

… During the last minute of her life she looked me with clarity in her eyes for the first time in three years. I know she knew me. She recognized my military uniform too. She smiled. Then she raised her head from her pillow and with all of the physical power left in her body she blew her final breath into my nostrils. She rested her head and closed her eyes.

"Mama", I said. "Mama! She's gone. She's gone!" I cried. As I wept, I told her, "I'll see you soon".

Mother, you're in heaven
And soon I will be there.
I'll see your smiling face again
And hear that happy belly laugh.
You and Daddy are waiting for me
While you're seated
at the foot of the throne.
Your legacy of evangelism
Still lives on.

As I held her in my arms, I heard sniffles behind me. I was not aware of the presence of the nurses and doctors at the foot of the bed who had been crying. I asked them, "Did you see her pass the blessing on to me - her second child of four? Oh how I wish the others were here."

I removed her Bible from her bedside stand and left to make memorial arrangements. When I drove away from the Mental Hospital, it was the most difficult drive I ever had to make.

Becky Dewitt

Author, Becky DeWitt is an inspiring author who captures ones' attention as she speaks from experience. She has published four books with Brentwood Christian Press, with the latest, *" Lips-Sacred or Scarred; Take Your Mouth Off The Mess and Use It For A Miracle",* receiving a review on the Publisher's Review Page. As a Christian author, her writings reveal trials and tribulations as well as edification to the soul. Her books express the need to talk about Jesus Christ from the ordinary everyday perspective with titles that are uncommon and the cover art as well. Becky lives and works in the Grand Strand Community.

The Vision You Can't See

Ladies and Gentlemen, announcing the one and only, the great work of God, marvelously and wonderfully made, You! Who me? Yes, You! A vessel that has been fashioned by God with greatness as a precious jewel, lying deeply embedded within, that is rich and curiously made. Take time to research who you are what you possess within as you carry the Word of God. Please understand, that you are not on this planet by accident or a mere random occurrence of birth. There is a purpose and plan for your life. You are a reservoir, holding much to be released.

CHOSEN For those of you who are a part of the RF (remnant factor), people who are reserved for special purpose at the appropriate time, God knew you and formed you in the belly before you came out of the womb. (Jeremiah 1:5). Please be advised that you are a chosen instrument, a part of an elite force, that He has separated and ordained for His purpose, not yours! He knew you in the spirit before you were wrapped in flesh. To know you, is to be intimate with you, meaning that He walked and talked with you, giving you specific instructions. As He is the Creator, there is treasure that He placed within you that you are not even aware of.

ANNOUNCEMENT Study to be quiet. Learn to keep the secrets that God gives you. That is why it is called a secret. He will only trust you with what He knows that you can handle. Just to let you know, everybody in the Body of Christ is not for you. Let's be real! If you want to test the waters, share the secret vision that God gave you about what He was going to do and see what happens. Remember Joseph shared his dreams with his brothers and ended up in the pit, although God made a way to the palace. The secret, the promise is unto for you to add to your faith, "that your faith should not stand in the wisdom of men, but in the power of God." (I Corinthians 2:5). You must understand that there are dreamcatchers and dreambusters. Dreamcatchers will listen and steal you dream and run with it before you know it. Dreambusters will speak all the impossibilities of the manifestation, sowing seeds of doubt into your mind that will eventually drop into the womb of your heart, if you allow your ears to continue to tune into the frequency of their mouth. Carry the vision in your heart until the appointed time to birth, to be released into the atmosphere. Remember Paul and some of the things that he saw, which could not be spoken. (2 Corinthians 12:4).

ENCOURAGEMENT Don't look for it. It will not come from your brothers and sisters in the Body of Christ, or even your Pastor. If it does, great. But remember it is *your* vision, *your* responsibility. You have to encourage yourself by holding to the vision that God gave you no matter what it looks or feels like. Keep it before the gates of your eyes and ears, knowing in your heart that it shall come to pass. In I Samuel 30:6, after David went through a great trial, the word says, "but David encouraged himself in the Lord, his God." This is just the beginning, the tip of the iceberg of your destiny. Add "keep the fire in and on my faith" to your job description through prayer, praise, and worship.

REJOICE Hallelujah! It is here! Praise the Lord! Glory to God! You have given birth to the vision. Stop. Look. Listen. Are you the only one giving praise for the blessing? Now watch this. Many will rejoice with a stranger, who they do not know, rather than rejoice with you, whom they know, and saw every step of the trial of your faith that it took to birth the vision. Do we lack the knowledge in knowing that if we rejoice in another man's blessing, adding our praise and worship with his, that as it goes up, the Father will smell the scent of fragrance of not only our lips, but our heart. Could it be the seed that is needed as you are in expectation for an uncommon harvest? As we know God is no respecter of persons. (Acts 10:34). If He did for you, then He can do it for me.

FULFILLMENT Have you ever thought that the Lord is coming back for the vision that He placed within you? Recently I heard a message that made me realize that I cannot afford to waste His time and gifts. In Matthew 25, the parable of the talents, examines how we must be prepared to execute the tasks (gifts) that are entrusted to us that produce results (fruit) for the kingdom.

In 1999, I published my first book, ***"The Three E's of Faith: Examine, Exercise, and Elevate***." Not exactly an easy topic to start with for one's first publication. As I have stayed on the potter's wheel, the process has produced three other books. Last year, the seed (thought), came to me about writing articles. It dropped into my heart (womb) and what you are reading is the second step of faith utilizing and multiplying ***that*** which I have been entrusted with. It is important that we be diligent in seeking the treasures in the realm of the spirit that the Father has hidden for our use as vessels, so that they will be manifested in the natural. Be faithful with what has been entrusted to you. Let Him see you "doing". After He has completed the forming and filling, let it flow.

"Though thy beginning was small, yet thy latter end should greatly increase." (Job 8:7).

James Murray

Vice-President, Elder, Director, Poet, and Aspiring Author is Mr. Murray, a South Carolina native, who was raised in the New Jersey and New York area. He graduated from The Stony Brook School on Long Island, NY and has a Bachelor of Science degree in Organizational Management from Morris College in Sumter, SC. He has two daughters, LT. April Tyler and Alexis. He is Vice-President of Columbia's Writers Alliance, who motivates youth and adults to live out their potential and discover their purpose in life. James is also an ordained Elder and Adult Bible Study leader serving at God's Church of Deliverance in Columbia, SC. He is a volunteer Chaplain/Pastor at an Alternative youth facility, Camp Aspen. Mr. Murray now serves as Prison Fellowship's Field Director-South Carolina. . He is a speaker for Lexington and Richland County Alcohol and Drug Abuse Council for which he received the United Way of the Midlands Direct Volunteer Service Award for 2001. All literary contributions are excerpts from his forthcoming book, "Rivers, Streams and Tributaries: A collection of poetry by James Murray."

Where Two Lines Meet

While riding down a country road,
    I passed through a one light town.
And as one does when driving,
    I casually looked around.
By a store, I saw some brothers (yea, my people)
   on the corner of a building chillin'.
Now a thought occurred, fixed in my mind my people can be found in any U.S. city or town
on some corner standing around, even sitting, singing, selling, yelling,
preaching, fortune telling or just lying down!
My people (yea, my people) on the corner, any corner there they'll be, even if there is no street.
At the tip of a square you'll find seven, nine, one or three; the corner of a lot, a building, a room; the corner where they take the three-point shot -- where Spike Lee does his shout-out.
The corner of a porch, a stair, wherever two perpendicular lines meet, my people on a corner there they'll be!
Why not the center, the middle, on a curve or top of a hill?
Just a question being asked, just like you might say,
"Hey, man what's your point?," I'm not yet sure.
I just seem to find my people (yea, my people) on the corner in any U.S. city or town. There they can be found.

You know it takes four lines to make a square.
Geometrically, when two lines meet they do make a point.

My people (yea, my people) in any U.S. city or town, on a corner can be found.

They gather together on a corner, anywhere, at the tip of a square.

Are they going somewhere?
Or do my people (yea, my people) like to be where two lines meet to make a point!
Man, you sound like you are on a negative trip!
Have you considered your people (yea, your people) are on the corner just waiting for the light to change or things to change so they can simply crossover to the other side?
True dat, true dat!
My people, (yea, my people)
Here's a truth God would have you to consider.
He sent a light for all to change. This light was crucified where two perpendicular lines meet.
"My people," God says. "Yes, my people, in any U.S. city or town, who on a corner can be found , who gather together on a corner anywhere at the tip of a square.
You can find grace, salvation, redemption and victory there; crossover and really go somewhere.
A place where two lines meet,
A simple cross to make a point! Selah.

Inspiration

When I hear you recite,
WOW!
I can't resist the urge to write.
The words explode into the air,
Enter my ear,

Entice the nerves,

Ignite my emotions to burn.
It’s a bubbling, churning,
passionate, yearning to express the song in my heart.
When I hear the poetry you recite,
Sister, brother, I can't resist the urge
To write!

Crimson Flower

Exquisite flower, beautiful to admire,
Fragrance armies have waged war to possess.
The petals are velvet. Its stem is thorny,
Sharp edges equipped to protect the sacredness of the flower.
Its color once was extremely bright, a pure white.
There is a rainbow of colors,
But white was the flower's right!
Until the day the thorny stems were fashioned
Into a crown!

To mock the King, the world ringed the thorns

And on His head they pressed them down! The BLOOD
Drained onto His face, His neck, from His hands
Across His chest, from His side,
Along His legs and His feet. The BLOOD
Stained the cross, the robe, the road and the ground!
Also stained all those who stood around,
The whole world then and now! The BLOOD
Penetrated our hearts, the stem, our minds,
The thorns and the petals of the Flower! The KING'S BLOOD

Has pierced many hearts from that hour to this hour!
This Crimson Flower reminds me

THE BLOOD HAS NEVER LOST ITS POWER!

Living Water

I am rooted; I am supported, sustained by this River.
Yes, the River of Living Water.

This river flows through my being, inhabits my body,
the source of my strength,
the power to abide by His will.

Without the River's nourishment, I would die, wither away,
shrink to nothing--a nobody,
an empty shell with no purpose, no vision, no life;
tossed about on waves in the sea of life;
living daily in sin and strife.

Thank you, gracious Jesus,
The Son of the Father,
for purchasing my rights
to the River of Living Water.

I am a branch in the True Vine;
a nature that is truly divine.

Blessings

Cold, cloudy days cause a man to enter into a deep,
depressive, meditative state.
Balmy days that cloak the sun, and darken nights that veil
the moon
Burden a man with remembrance of squandered blessings
gone by.
One anticipates the renourishing radiance of the sun and the
refreshing luminance of the moon, which provide blessings
to come.
When the sun shines and showers him with light, he
scurries for shade and shelter;
and complains about the brilliance of this blessed event.
When the moon is full of glory and illuminates the night,
and exposes all shadows of the night,
Man sleeps and slumbers during this blessed event.
As it is with our souls and God;
But if a soul repents, he bathes in the radiance; basks in the
luminance.

The War With No Name
(Formerly a Psalm for Anthony Reardon)

Those who have ears, let them hear, more soldiers have
been slain in the war with no name.
Their blood was shed in a war without
a cause or a land claim.
More soldiers have been slain.
Do they die in vain?
I ask you, Brothers, Mothers, Sisters, Fathers,
Sons and Daughters,
"Do you know the cause for which they were slain?
Could you tell me, please, this warfare's name?"
Martin knew the cause for which he was slain; Malcolm,
Medgar, Marcus, Crispus, Hannibal and Shaka knew the
cause for which they were slain.

Did they die in vain?
I mean every war has a name or some kind of claim.
These brothers and soldiers were slain.
Tell me, please, what is this war's name?
To those who carry a gun in this war with no name,
your brothers' blood cries in the hip-hop game!
What is the cause or claim for which we were slain?
Please, tell me, what is this war's name?
Did we die in vain for a war with no name?
I hear Mothers weeping for their sons and daughters.
Why are they being slain and what is this war's name?
Those who have ears take heed what you hear.
There were those who were slain for a cause, definitely a
Name above all names.
Peter, Paul and John knew the cause for which they were
slain. They did not die in vain.
Stephen knew the Name, **JESUS.**

He was slain and His blood was shed in a
war with a cause, a most serious claim.
His blood cries out, "It is finished, it is done,"
especially to those who carry a gun, in a war with no name,
in the hip-hop game, fighting and being slain,
dying in vain.

His blood speaks louder than TUPAC and B.I.G.
Come fight in this war and truly overcome.
And if you are slain, no death is in vain.
For to live is Christ, to die is gain, in the war of faith for
the Name above all names!

My Brothers, Sisters, Mothers, Fathers, Sons and
Daughters, don't fight in a war which has no name.
Fight the good fight of faith for the Name above all names!
And our Brothers' deaths shall not be in vain! SELAH!

The Real (Man Power)

(For TD Jakes and Manpower Ministry)

The world keeps saying,
“A sea of men, a sea of black men.”

“A wave of pride” is what it cries

A sea of a million black men has come to the hill.
The world does not see nor can it perceive the power of the real.
He who stands on the shore and calls and draws the men named a sea.
He is false, he only stands to deceive.
He sees power in the sea, a million wide, a wave of pride to blot away the dunes
built to protect a society of
sensual pleasure and prominence.
But he does not see THE REAL!
He calls a day of atonement excluding him, who has atoned.
Everyone says, "Wow!"
What a sea, such a wave of pride.
A sea of a million black men has come to the hill. Does anyone see the real?
Take courage my brother, I saw the real!
A remnant south of the hill, a current of meekness, an undertow in the flow.

Where "Eyes have not seen or ears have not heard, nor entered into the hearts" what God
Has for the black man; POWER!
THE REAL, my brother, HAS BEEN REVEALED!
look deep, deep beneath the wave of pride and the sea of a million men.
South of the hill. there was a remnant, a current of meekness, an undertow in the flow
where they praise, pray and preach in the name of
THE ATONEMENT. THE REAL.
T.D. stood on a shore (south of the hill) chosen and he called a remnant of men who drew from THE REAL.
And in His name , they will tear down the dunes protecting the society of sin which thrives beyond the shore.
The real remnant, a current of meekness, the undertow in the flow will wash away the dunes into the sea of no more.

My Shoppe!
(For Sister Joan Huiett)

Today was a good day to go shopping,
Not so much to buy, just to watch!
Walk the avenue, gaze into the windows,
Observe what they had to offer,
Imagine how it should be to own my Shoppe!
The first window, I gazed into
displayed fine linen and silk dresses,
Tailored for praise!

Imagine being escorted before the King,
clothed in one of these fine garments!
The sign over the window read
Garments of Praise!
I admired the owner and would enjoy wearing the praise,
However I knew this shoppe would not be mine!
Next door,
I observed and watch on display instruments and melody
makers
All shapes and sizes!
I could hear the song ring in my head,
"Praise Him all Creatures here below!"
"Praise Him above the heavenly Host!:
"Praise the Father, Son and Holy Ghost!"
The Scriptures says,
Praise Him with All the instruments!"
The sign read,
"Making Melody"
Yes, it is what would I do, but it is not what I would sell!
The next window was empty; nothing on display the sign
had no words in the frame,

The shop had no name!
And before I could ask why, I heard Him say, “This one’s yours”!
I replied, “I never imagined this to be”,
and
He said,” What ever you imagine, it will be!”
Before I blinked or batted my eye,
The window was filled with the finest china and gold goblets and silver settings on tables draped with silk table-cloths!
The walls were plagued with landscape paintings more real than life!
I walk through the entrance into a grand hall, decked for a banquet!
A grand feast was prepared to be served,
The aroma satisfied any appetite I thought I had or ever could have!
The King said to be me, “This is the place I have designed for you,
A place for you to serve, welcome people to dine with the King!”
I danced and whirled and pranced and whirled and praise him until I melodically move from the back of the room to the entrance again!
I went out the door from the shoppe that I knew was mine and looked up at the sign!
Heavenly Hospitality!

Sonja Williams

Sonja T. Williams is the author of the children's book entitled Aloma and the Red Suitcase. The brilliantly illustrated book is for elementary-age readers. It tells a wonderful story about an eight-year-old girl that is momentarily devastated when she learns that she is moving across country leaving her best friend behind. The young girl learns about the value of friendship and responsibility.

Sonja T. Williams is an active member of the Society of Children's Book Writers and Illustrators. Additionally, she is a member of the Columbia Writers Alliance where she serves as Treasurer. She is an advocate of children's literacy and believes that learning to read is critical for success in school and later on in life. She hopes that parents and guardians help foster the joy of reading by reading to their children at an early age. Sonja resides in Columbia, South Carolina with her family. She is currently working on two additional projects.

Reader Bee

I read daily because
it's important to me.
I go to the library
with my family.
Once inside we
scatter around.
There are so many
books to be found.
The walls are lined with
book after book.
I grab a bunch and
settle in a nook.
I read and read
for hours at a time,
And my parents,
they don't mind.
Because I'm doing something
important you see.
I'm reading a book; I'm a reader bee.
So go to the library and take a look.
Curl up, get cozy and read a book!

Imagination

I travel to places
near and far,
And I don't even
have to get in a car.

I use my
imagination to take
me away
To exciting places
just for a day.

You too can go on exciting trips.
I've been to the circus and
on a cruise ship!
I just use my imagination
to take me there,
And I'm riding an elephant while
balancing a chair.

Go ahead, use your imagination
and you will see
What a fantastic voyage it will be.
I'll make you a promise;
I'll promise you this,
It's one trip you won't want to miss.

Loving Her

I watch her in silence from across the room,
Angry, confused – don't know what to do.

This thing is creeping into her life
Turning everything upside down,
Toying with her mind
Seizing precious moments — our time.

Gone are the talks on the phone
For what seems like hours,
This sickness is grabbing hold of her
Claiming her power.

Her power to think and be free
Or maybe her power's unbroken and it's just me
Caught up in the rapture of what's supposed to be.

So what do I do I ask myself?
Do I treat her the same or like
she's somebody else?

She looks like the person I've known all my life.
She's still a mom, a grandma, a wife.

Do I have a temper tantrum?
Throw my hands up in despair?
'Cause I just can't take it
And no one seems to care.

Do I hold a pity party?
Stop hoping things will change?
'Cause I've given up the fight
Believing life won't be the same.

What do I do I ask myself?
I stare at her in the mirror.
And the answer comes with the blink of an eye,
You just love her…you just love her.

Eyes Listening

Lips parted
My words flow eloquently
His eyes fix on me
And I'm elated you see
So my words flow on and on
Like a child with exciting news of the day
Like my favorite song on instant replay

His eyes are fixed on me
Except I realize he's gone
His mind that is
To the game, last night, perhaps yesterday
He's just gone to another time and place
I long for his eyes to see the look on his face

His eyes are fixed on me
But just for a minute
'Cause his mind, his soul isn't in it
The moment that is, when my words flow
Flow eloquently from my lips
Like a child with exciting news of the day
Like my favorite song on instant replay

Allen Watkins

Aspiring Novelist, Songwriter. Mr. Watkins resides in Winnsboro, SC. He is married and works as a sub teacher at Winnsboro Technology Center. Mr. Watkins has 2 manuscripts ready for publication. He is a graduate of WV State and enjoys playing tennis.

The Vital Spark

Preface

Coming Soon to a Book Store Near You! A Novel entitled *The Vital Spark*

The novel is aimed at adults who like foreign intrigue with a bit of murder sandwiched between and a lot of science fiction that's rapidly becoming fact.

The novel takes place primarily in Bethesda, Maryland and its surrounding communities where life is created in a research lab from off the shelf chemicals but a home grown heart might steal the show.

Third Reich Resurrectionist, (Neo Nazis) aim to steal the patent to once again raise its ugly head ever trying to create the master race. Does the world have to fight these guys again?

The Vital Spark (an excerpt)

Chapter I

Dr. Frazer turned and walked the short distance from the cluttered test tube table to the dark grey, well-polished granite top counter that stretched from one end of the research lab's wall to the other. She then cautiously inserted a drill bit twice the circumference of a human hair follicle, locked it in, pulled the on switch and began to quickly drill several holes in the transparent half-inch thick plastic lid that was about the size that would cover a bread box. Shortly after, she placed it over the top of the well-constructed glass box containing what resembled a pinkish brown mud puddle, one-quarter the size of a penny with an almost microscopic piece of grey matter that could only be described as looking like a minute speck of play dough shaped like an earthworm.

"I guess it's time we tell somebody about this," she said, motioning to her two leading research assistants as they followed her down the freshly waxed and buffed hallway leading to their corporate offices wearing their soiled white smocks.

"We've been up for over 48 hours," she complained.

“We must get some rest, but not until we let Dr. Gatlin know what we’ve done. I want the ethicist to get ahead of this thing,” she said, pulling back the unkempt long blonde strands of hair that totally covered her right eye while jamming her left balled up fist into her smock's pocket as they entered the doorway to the office manager's plush, thickly carpeted suite.

Send a night letter to Gatlin, she dictated, leaning over the office manager's coffee-stained mahogany desk, pulling her bifocals down over her nose. "Tell him that chemical information in the form of gene number299 was the 'vital spark.' Make him understand that seconds after we dropped gene number 299 in the test tube's liquid, micro-plasma genetalium's lifeless matter began to swim. It virtually came alive."

She turned to her two leading researchers. "Do you guys have anything to add?"

"Yes," Bill Ventura conceded, twisting a little to one side. "Tell him that several hours later we dropped in gene number 300 and it excreted waste."

"Yeah," said Jim Tonic, the third researcher, leaning against the wall with his foot propped against its bottom. "Tell him that still a few hours later we dropped in gene number 301 and the organism floated to the surface of the liquid as if gasping for air. Tell him that we then took it out of the test tube and laid it in a puddle on the bottom of a clear glass box and it continues to live and breathe. We surmise that it is amphibious and that it has grown from a microscopic bacterium to one-sixteenth the size of a fishing worm in about 24 hours." "Tell him we've stopped all research and that we will not add another gene until we hear from him and the panel," said Dr. Frazer.

"By the way, guys, let's go get some sleep," she added as they left the office heading for the snow-covered parking lot.

"Son-of-a-gun," the young office manager Eddie Smith exclaimed loudly, leaning back in his heavily padded leather chair." "I wish they had given this friging task to you," he sobbed swiveling his chair, turning to his personal secretary then standing up to expose his six foot two frame and his monogrammed gold cuff links matching the gold buttons on his dark navy blue sports jacket, unconsciously spilling a little coffee on the plush carpet.

"You know, I've been known as quite the agnostic around town and now I've got to write the most noted bioethecist in the country telling him that God may be right here at 29111 and Mohawk Streets in Bethesda, Maryland

and that he's not singular, in fact he's three people and headed up by a she that's a blonde, 26 year old, tall, good looking white woman; a short, 28 year old white man of Italian descent and a 23 year old, near six-foot black guy from Selma Alabama nonetheless. Damn, all hell's about to break loose around here," Eddie exclaimed. "I'm glad they gave you the task," Julie replied, "I want no part of this if I can help it," she sighed. "It's not the genie out of the bottle, it's the gene literally out of the bottle and I'm not sure Gatlin can keep the lid on it. You know his panel consists of ministers, ethicists, philosophers, doctors and lawyers and I've never known a lawyer who wouldn't leak a secret. Besides, you've been on the wrong side of your dad down in Georgia for a long time with his congregation up in arms about your agnosticism. This blasphemy of yours, as he puts it, is really going to piss him off now, when he discovers that you're an integral part of this thing. Don't be surprised if he and his congregation don't march right up here and picket the hell right out of this place," Julie said. "Besides, I've got a date tonight," she added, standing up, putting on her overcoat. "See yuh," she continued in her heavy South African accent rushing out of the office into the back parking lot.

Eddie laid his arm on his favorite padded leather chair

and looked out the stained glass window. He watched until Julie Tomarrow had left the slippery parking lot. "She had a hard time getting traction in the snow," he thought, sitting back down, pondering over the selection of words he'd have to write Dr. Gatlin.

"I'll keep it simple," he thought, as he began to type the words on his PC.

"Dear Dr. Gatlin, Fay Frazer, Bill Ventura and Jim Tonic have asked me to relay some startling information, requesting that you convene your panel as soon as possible on the following and let us know what problems we're apt to encounter when the below information becomes public."

"Late last night they dropped informational chemistry in the form of gene number 299 into a bit of lifeless matter. That lifeless matter was the off the shelf chemical components known to have been contained in the make up of a parasitic bacterium known as microplasma genetalium. When the researchers dropped in informational chemistry known as gene number 299, the lifeless matter virtually came to life in the test tube. Subsequently, they dropped in informational chemistry known as gene number 300 and the now-living parasite began to excrete body waste. Later, they dropped in chemistry known as gene number 30 I and the living organism floated to the surface of the test tube as if gasping for air. They took it out of the test tube's liquid, placed it in a puddle in a glass box and it continues to live, showing signs of being amphibious. The team has elected to cease all research as agreed until they hear from you and your panel. If you have questions, please let me know."

Reading his freshly written letter aloud to himself, Eddie Smith managed a slight smile and seemed to be satisfied that he had chosen the proper words. He pulled a Federal Express envelope from his desk drawer, inserted the letter and walked across the street to the FedEx office.

"Hello Mr. Smith," the Federal Express counter girl said. "Haven't seen you in for a while."

Eddie did not respond as he handed the letter to the counter girl. Finally, smiling, he replied, "Jane, I need this delivered by 10AM in the morning please. It's very important. Oh, and forgive me for not speaking, guess I was just a. little preoccupied," Eddie added as he slammed the door, walked back across the street around to the parking lot and drove off down the street in his 4X4 to the Holiday Inn's cocktail lounge just four blocks away.

"Gimme a double Jack on the rocks," he told the bartender.

"A double," Sheila repeated, "Are you going to tie one on this evening?"

"I don't think so," Eddie replied, "1 don't have a designated driver. I just need a quick nerve numbing substance to settle me down a little!"

"I agree," the bartender replied. "You're very ashy, you look like you've seen a ghost."

"On the contrary," Eddie exclaimed, turning the bourbon up and downing it all at once. "I've seen a ghost come to life and he's only the size of a pin head."

Sheila smiled, dismissed Eddie's reply as some kind of offbeat sarcasm, blew her nose in a bar napkin and waited on another customer. Eddie wondered if she had a cold, hoping he wouldn't catch it, when suddenly there was a tap on his shoulder. He turned slightly.

"Julie?" he questioned, "Thought you had a hot date for the evening?"

"I thought I did too." She exclaimed. "But when I got to the condo, I didn't really feel that 1'd be good company on a date tonight, so I canceled. To be honest, I feel more like having a few drinks with my friends," she said. "Oh, come on Eddie, let's sit over in the comer," she added, motioning him to follow.

"OK," he said, while turning to Sheila, ordering another drink for himself and Julie.

It was after the jazz combo had played its first song before either one of them spoke again.

"You know, it wouldn't be so bad if they had seemed excited or something when they came into the office and dropped the big bomb, huh." I mean, they were so damn casual' about it. You'd think they'd be dancing for joy or crying or something human, you know?"

"Yes, I know," said Julie. "You'd think those fuckers would have been flying high, instead they broke the news and said they were going to sleep." How the hell can they sleep at a time like this? They're pure sausage," she lamented.

"The problem is that if you look at the big picture, man himself has only 80,000 or so genes. Hell, it won't take Bear, I mean that Super Computer down the hall calculating information at the speed of light to figure out the sequence and string together the order of man's entire genetic repertoire. I don't have to tell you what that implies," Eddie said.

"This is almost frightening," Julie added.

"You damn right!" Eddie said. "And once it happens, there will be no turning back. That creature down there in the lab right now is as simple as a life form can be, but it is still life. Hell, the microplasma genetalium has only 470 genes in its entire genetic repertoire to begin with. They took away 170 before the thing became lifeless matter, then they duplicated the matter with off the shelf chemicals. Concluding that it really needed only 300 of its 470 original genes to actually live.

"You're so right," a voice spoke from the dimly lit opposite corner of the lounge, becoming stronger as their bodies moved closer to Eddie's table. It was Bill Ventura and Jim Tonic.

"How long you guys been here," Eddie asked?

"About ten minutes," Bill Ventura replied quickly as Jim Tonic looked at his watch.

"Yea, about ten, he second. "We thought we could sleep too but we couldn't," they said sitting down at the table beside Eddie and Julie.

'" Let's get some hamburgers, I'm starved," Julie suggested in her heavy South African accent.

Julie Tomarrow carried a lot of clout around M&L Labs. She was a transplant from the strife-ridden P.W. Botha regime. Although she was classified as 'colored', which meant that their skin was generally light brown, and were usually better educated and were given better jobs than most black South Africans. They were among the segregated underclass and needed a pass when going from town to town as did the black South Africans. Johannesburg, where Julie was born, kept a tight watch on educated coloreds, especially like Julie who was known to be a card carrying member of the free Mandella movement. Julie was truly beautiful, standing almost six feet tall and full of charm. She had worked for a large US corporation whose home base was St. Paul, Minnesota and had offices and manufacturing in Johannesburg before coming to the US on a Visa. Actually the South African government was glad to get rid of her as they put it. Julie had been long since classified ever since her college days (is a dissident. Openly pro- Mandella with ties to the ANC. She had a short marriage to a young white corporate executive doing a tour of duty for his Minnesota home based company. He returned to St. Paul with Julie and they were actually married for six months, but their marriage fell apart when the young executive's father denounced him, changed his will and threatened to leave the young executive $1.00 out of a $50 million inheritance. Julie convinced the young executive that she did not love him and that Minnesota was too cold a climate for her anyway. The marriage was dissolved as the young executive declared he'd marry her again as soon as his ailing father passed away. He advised Julie to take the $500,000 offered her by his parents. She did, leaving Minnesota for Washington, DC. She set up in a condo in Bethesda and landed a secretarial job at M&L Labs, for which she was overqualified. Julie was highly skilled as a receptionist and secretary. She's a class act. The M&L customers would complement her management.

"She's efficient, kind and a pleasure to do business with," they'd say.

"I'll pay for the hamburgers," another voice said coming from the direction of the bar. They all turned to see Fay Frazer headed over to the table with a tray of drinks.

"Damn," Eddie said "Wait, don't tell me. You couldn't sleep either?"

"You're right." Dr. Frazer replied sitting the drinks down on the table. I guess we all were just fooling ourselves except you Eddie."

"Hell, I'm just glad to know you guys are human after all," he said happily.

“So you think we're a little laid back about this thing, hum Eddie?" Fay Frazer asked.

"It's just that you did seem a bit nonchalant," Eddie replied.

"Well you can rest assured that we're not," she said smiling. I never doubted the social gravity of the work being done at M&L Labs. It's just that there's always a social lag between science and society as a whole. Science almost always out strips sociality, leaving it somewhere behind, scrambling to catch up. Leap frog technology enables science to make new and profound discoveries in a much shorter time frame now as opposed to the old days. These new discoveries are pushing society to make decisions about the origin of the species and about life or its beginning much more often."

"A verse well spoken," Julie added, cutting Dr Frazer off in the middle of her dissertation. "So we'll wait till the panel sends us their opinion before we proceed down this slippery slope, huh?" Julie said with tongue and cheek.

Dr. Bill Ventura and Dr. Frazer both broke out into

a conservative laugh, as they downed their drinks and motioned to the waitress for another round.

Eddie Smith leaned back in his chair, interlocked his fingers behind his head, and then turned toward Fay.

"I've sent Dr. Gatlin the night letter," he whispered. "He should have it by 10am tomorrow. He'll have all weekend to discuss the subject with his panel. I left my home number in case he needs further clarification."

"'-Very well," replied Fay. "Now enough about our research. Let's have some fun now while we can," she exclaimed as the little jazz band started to play.

"Your love is like an alabaster palace, warmer than the midnight sun," the attractive vocalist sang.

"By the way," Dr. Ventura asked. "Did anyone go back to the lab, cover up the microplasma and turn out the lights? It's not to be exposed to light or radiation of any kind for more than eight hours at a time. I believe Jim proved that when he noted a slight tropism after about seven hours in the light, which leads me to believe that radiation even in small doses could change its genetic structure and cause us some unforeseen problems by Monday. That song reminded me you know, 'The Midnight Sun.'"

"You could be right Bill," Fay replied. "Say Jim, the

lab's on your way back to your condo, could you possibly stop by and turn the lights off or cover it up?"

"I'll do both," Jim said. "No problem, I've got the weekend watch anyway, so I'll get going."

"OK Jim," Fay replied as she helped him with his jacket, then patted him on the back as she watched him disappear from the doorway and into the cold, clear February night.

Some employees at M&L Labs were envious of the relationship between Dr. Frazer and Jim Tonic. He seemed to be able to do what ever he wanted around the lab without punity. What ever he asked for, Fay would always approve without question. Jim Tonic was a no-nonsense researcher and a young southern gentleman. In fact, Fay hired him at the bottom of the stage as he walked off in cap and gown on his graduation day from Johns Hopkins. He was valedictorian of the class, majoring in chemistry but did his thesis in genetics, his minor. She later interviewed him with his mother at his side. Jim's father was a cotton field straw boss outside Selma Alabama but his mother, determined to get him a good education, worked for a wealthy white couple as a nanny for years. Jim grew up independent and aggressive. Fay and Bill Ventura had met Jim Tonic when they gave a seminar over at Johns Hopkins. When they asked the class of their intentions, most said they wanted to get with a lab who had a government grant to fund their research in various disciplines after graduation but Jim Tonic said he felt he was good enough to take his chances with a private lab. He said he didn't need a hand out or a safety net but needed only a hand up, and that he wanted to be free of the regimentation of government funded research. This answer impressed Bill Ventura and Fay Frazer, along with his straight A average, because Bill Ventura and Dr. Frazer had vowed to beat the government funded labs to take the lead in genome structures. Jim Tonic had also displayed leadership being an all-conference quarterback in school, electing to cast his lot in science instead of football.

"'That's the kind of personnel we want," Fay had said at the end of the seminar. "Let's try him out in June after he graduates." She explained to Bill on their way back to the M&L Labs.

"He could be what we're looking for. He's young bright and a minority to boot. He'll look good on our EEO paperwork when we go for government contracts," Bill added.

"Does anyone care to dance?" Julie asked as the band played another selection.

"I think I've had it for the evening," Eddie Smith said. "I don't have that designated driver," he added.

"And neither do we," Bill Ventura second.

"Well that settles it," Fay interrupted. "Shall we go home, 1 believe 1 can sleep now."

It was 10 AM by the time Jim Tonic got to the lab. He stopped by at 11 PM the night before to turn the lights out and cover up the microplasma, as promised.

"This place seems a bit eerie when no one's in the lab," he thought. "It's nice of M&L Labs to allow Lincoln's birthday as a holiday," he said aloud, turning on the lights and pulling off the cloth that covered the glass box containing the microplasma. Jim placed his portable electronic microscope over the microplasma. He seemed a bit perturbed. Then released the microscope and headed for the phone.

"Fay Frazer please," he asked.

"Just a minute," a female voice replied. "She's just coming out of the shower."

"Good morning Dr. Frazer," Jim Tonic said. "I'm at the lab. I covered the genetalium up last night and noticed no change but this morning at 10: 15 the microplasma has grown one half centimeter according to the sizeometer. I'm looking at something that was microscopic 24 hours ago to something one-half the size of a M&M candy pellet, except it has a tail that looks like a tadpole and seems as comfortable out of the liquid puddle as it does in it. It's definitely amphibious."

"I wouldn't be alarmed at the early accelerated growth the first 24 hours," said Dr. Frazer. "It's natural for parasitic bacterium that is exposed to high amounts of oxygen level as in the human environment to grow rapidly for the first24 to 48 hours. Cover it up, turn out the lights and take the afternoon off. Security is on duty."

"'1 just saw security check the door," Jim replied.

"'OK, then lock the lab door. We don't want to take a chance of someone accidentally knocking it over.

"'Just a few more things before you leave, Jim." Fay asked. Will you look on Julie's desk and quickly review my paper. It's the one entitled *"The Genome Sequence of the Bacteria That Causes Syphilis".* It's the one I'll be presenting tomorrow in Geneva, but don't disturb Bill's paper on the etiology of Lyme Disease. You know how he is when he feels that someone's looking over his shoulder. Make any corrections on mine that you feel necessary and don't forget to complete your paper on ulcers, but don't let it interfere with your travel plans to pick up the blood sampling from the Cameroonian prostitute who's known to be immune to HIV. Make sure you have two witnesses while you draw her blood. Be prepared to pay her a thousand dollars. We may need her again when we start to sequence her HIV antibodies. The concord leaves from Dulles Airport at two p.m. Bill and I will stop by and pick up our papers on the way. See you when we get back.

Chapter 2

Jim Tonic hung the phone up, "I've got quite a bit to do in the next few weeks," he thought as he covered the microplasma, turned out the lights and headed down the hall to review Fay's paper. He scanned the lO-page report, made a few grammatical corrections, and then went over to the secretarial pool desk to output the corrections. He pushed the *ON* key and a few seconds later noticed an ' undeleted e-mail message addressed to Rose McCarthy, the employee's desk at which he sat. "Ten thousand if you can get the genetic information on 'ME'," it said. "I know they're close, they may have already found 'the Vital Spark,' Delete."

Jim Tonic leaned back nervously, "What the hell's this all about," he thought. "Could it be that we have a corporate spy in our labs? I'll output this message first and save it for Fay. Then I'll go to another computer and do her paper. "

Jim unplugged the desktop, covered it with plastic and went over to Eddie's desk and quickly output the corrections.

"That message on Rose's e-mail has some grave implications. Somebody' s going down hard for a long time," he thought. "That desktop must have malfunctioned or they didn't know M&L Labs was off today." Jim Tonic folded the e-mail message, crossed his legs and quickly shoved it in his sock.

"It's too late," a voice said, setting at a compute(in the boiler room at NIH, some five blocks away. Someone has seen the message because it has been output and I'm not sure it was Rose. Whoever it was did not use our code."

"Y ou fool," the second voice said, "You should have called to make sure she was there first. You'll just have to go over there and take care of it."

"I'll wait for Fay," Jim thought. "She's got to know what's going on before she leaves for Geneva."

JimTonic heard footsteps coming down the hall. He put Fay's papers in a folder. "That's her now, I'll bet," he surmised as the office door cracked open. He looked up; there was a 32 caliber pistol with a silencer pointed at his head. A single shot was fired, piercing his forehead causing him to slump across the desk with blood dripping from his nose like a leaking faucet, making a red puddle on the cover of Dr. Fay Frazer's paper.

The lone gunman seemed to be all nerve with no regard for security and absent of remorse as he entered the office at a natural pace. Obviously familiar with the surroundings, he headed for the secretarial pool's desk placing a small packet of plastic explosives against the side panel of the desktop's monitor, slowly backing away, as there was a muffled sound of an explosion that completely destroyed the computer. A second later he glanced over at Jim Tonic's still body as he casually exited the building for the parking lot. Driving carefully, he turned right onto Mohawk Avenue, even pausing to tip his hat to Fay Frazer and Bill Ventura as they waited for the light to change in order to make the left turn to enter the campus of M& L Labs.

"My God!" said Fay Frazer as she led the way over to Jim Tonic's seemingly lifeless body, now bleeding profusely all over the desk. "Jim Tonic's been shot!" she cried holding his left arm trying to feel his pulse. "He's barely alive!" she exclaimed. "Call the ambulance, have them notify the police that there's been a shooting."

"And Rose's computer has been blown to bits," Bill Ventura added as Fay Frazer ripped off her white silk blouse unconsciously leaving herself bare breasted as she fashioned a tourniquet and tightly tied it around Jim Tonic's forehead.

Fay Frazer began to shiver from the shock in the cool low heated office as Bill Ventura threw his grey tweed sport coat about her shoulders.

"I believe 1 hear a siren in the distance," said Bill Ventura while Fay again checked the pulse of Jim Tonic. "He's got less than five minutes I figure," added Bill. "His breathing is much too shallow. First there will be shock, then cardiac arrest will follow soon unless he gets immediate life support, I'm afraid," he continued.

Suddenly the doors to the office flung open. Three paramedics entered hurriedly with a gurney in tow full of life support apparatus. By this time Jim Tonic had stopped breathing.

"He's comatose," one paramedic hollered as they laid Jim on the gurney placing two paddles on his chest and applying electricity intermittently as his pale chest rose and fell each time the power surged.

"We've go a heartbeat," one paramedic said as she hooked up the IV s and started to roll the gurney toward the now opened back fire door where the ambulance driver had parked the vehicle.

"Ask the police to lock the doors once the crime scene has been secured then you come on over to Bethesda Medical," Fay whispered to Bill Ventura. "'I'll have to cancel my trip. You might want to call Eddie and Julie before you come," she said solemnly. "You can catch a flight out later."

"Jim Tonic's been what?" replied Eddie Smith.

"Yea, he's been shot," Bill Ventura repeated. "He's clinging to life. The paramedics have him and they may already be at Bethesda Medical."

"I'll call Julie and come right over," Eddie Smith said excitedly.

Keisha Bass

Keisha Bass was born in Georgia and grew up in Harrisburg, Pennsylvania. She currently lives in Columbia, South Carolina with her husband and two children. This is her first children's book and she is currently working on her next book project. Keisha is currently a member of the Columbia Writers Alliance.

Searching

Searching

Trying to find what is missing

My life feels comfortable yet empty

Looking to see if I can put my finger on it

Still searching

For what is missing

One day Jesus came into my life

Now my life is complete

No longer searching for what was missing

Jesus took away that empty feeling

The Family Tree

It starts at the root where the tree begins
With proper nourishment and treatment the tree will never end
The branches start growing and start spreading their different ways,
Feeling their best on those sunny days.
Nevertheless, the sun has to go down as a breeze starts to blow
The branches have settled down and now are ready to grow

As the branches starts to grow and the leaves begin to form
With all different sizes and colors a beautiful tree is born
As the tree starts to grow and the branches starts to age
The tree has matured and seen a many of days
Then as time goes by and a couple of leaves begin to fall
Still yet, no matter what the tree stands tall
A branch may fall here and there knowing its time has come to leave
Still through the storm and rain no matter what still stands our tree

A tree is like life, as we know it today
When you plant a firm foundation, you will go a long way
So, as our tree continues to grow in our family
Remember where it started from and how it came to be

It was through our past that made us who we are
And for that we have a great deal to thank God for.

Memories

Precious pearls and diamond rings
Colorful rainbows that the evening brings
A sweet innocent whisper from the Ocean Sea
A touch of laughter in the spring breeze
Sometimes we wonder how life would be
If we did not have such memories

Smile

There is something so wonderful
and means so much to me
Giving someone a smile whoever they may be
It's something that takes less than
a minute for anyone to do
It warms the hearts of many and
mostly given by few
So when you see someone in a store, on the street or just
passing by
Remember what a smile would
mean given with a hi.

What Is Happening?

What is happening to our world today?
What is up with the anger, violence and rage?
What is the cause of all this pain?
Is it the self-destruction of asking,
who is to blame?
The drugs, the violence and the
killing on the streets
Will never get better, just make us weak
So we as people must be apart
Of changing this world, starting with our hearts
And if we as people don't come together as one
We will end up with a world
dangerous for everyone

Try Jesus

If you are looking for a change in your life

Try Jesus

If you are looking to make everything alright

Try Jesus

If you are looking for some peace within

Try Jesus

If you are looking for something better than the world of sin

Try Jesus

Jesus is knocking at your door

Open it and explore

Explore the world of how it's going to be

If you choose the life of eternity

The Disguise

While riding home from work, I saw an old lady carrying groceries alone
I pulled up beside her and asked, "Do you need a ride home?"
It seemed like she looked familiar as she got into the car
I asked her where did she live and she said not that far
She told me that her name was Faith and she did not mind walking alone
I was quite taken by her sincere tone
Somehow we started talking about the Lord openly
I told her some of the things that He has done for me
Then with a smile she said," God loves you."
I thought to myself, where did this come from out of the blue
Then she told me to turn right and go about three-forth of a mile
This is where I live she said as she smiled
She told me that everything happens for a reason, whatever it may be
She said remember my name, Faith, and what it means
She got out of the car and said we will meet again
When you least expect it, you will find me within
I looked in my rearview mirror as I started to drive

Faith had disappeared to my surprise

I heard that sincere voice saying, "Faith is something you have to believe in and nothing you can see."

The faith that I picked was really apart of me.

Little Angels

There are little angels all around waiting to show their love
Touching the lives of many, God has sent them from above
Always there to give a smile on a rainy day
Making you laugh sometimes with the things that they say
Showing their love so genuine and true
They are special blessings that are sent to you
So when you think of little angels, think of something dear
It's the little girls and boys, God has sent to cheer.

Grandmother

There is someone in my life
that means so much to me
She always there no matter

what and gives her love so freely
She Generates an atmosphere
that we all love to share

She Reaches out to others
when no one else is there
She Acknowledges anything
special to us-- whatever it maybe

She Never puts down our dreams
that we may want to reach
She Discuss our futures

and gives us her very best
She Motivates our thinking
with nothing but success

She Observes when we are happy
or sad or even when we pout
She Takes the time to explain
to us what life is all about
She Heals our wounded hearts
with her gentle smile

She Explains that love comes and goes and sometimes
stays for a little while
She is Respected by many and never by few
We love you GRANDMOTHER for all the things you do

Sharaledon D. Brave

A native of Georgetown, South Carolina, Sharaledon D. Brave is a poet, writer, artist and photographer . Sharaledon uses his talents to speak compassionately to and about his community. His freshman project, *What Will I Tell My Children* is a wonderfully, inspiring collection of poetry centered on the philosophy, "It takes a village to raise a child". Mr. Brave has also recently released a line of greeting cards with the slogan, *Say It With Love.* The greeting card line encompasses many of the wonderful poetry from *What Will I Tell My Children*

Mama Still Sings

I can still hear my mama singing
Her songs rest sweetly in my heart
Songs of faith and adoration
From which I will never part

I can still hear my mama singing
Each verse becoming her own
Humming a measure here and there
A testimony in her tone

I can still hear my mama singing
The refrain is bold and clear
Singing about that
Great getting-up-morning
Hoping to see you there

Mama's songs were from her heart
Fortified by God's grace
I can still hear my mama singing
Though I cannot see her face

I can still hear my mama singing
Her songs are tried and true
Faithful in the midst of storms
Her singing still brings me through

Beauty in Blackness

You take the beauty of blackness
To a much higher place
From the locks of your hair
To the contours of your face

You embrace the beauty of blackness
Like no one I've ever seen
While many cling to white as snow
You endorse black as sharp and clean

You ordain blackness as royalty
Honoring it with great respect
And whatever shares it common space
In itself becomes a precious object

Keep taking your blackness higher
Creating your personal plane
Someday all will appreciate your blackness
Even if they have forgotten your name

My Dwelling Place

Father, You are my dwelling place
The sunrays upon my face
The wind against my back
The light between the cracks

The promise in time of storm
That I'll never be left alone
The anointing upon my head
By grace and mercy I am led

You are my counselor
Touching my eyelids with sleep
You are my very best friend
For my secrets You do keep

You are my way-maker
When mountain are all I see
You are the King of Glory
Who sets my shackles free

When others try to trouble me
As I continue to run this race
I shall keep on keeping on
For You are my dwelling place

Grandma's Gift

As I exercise my right
To rejoice with a soul set free
I know it was made possible
Because somebody prayed for me

I know I didn't ask
For God to bring me through
I was too busy in this world
Grandmother, was it you?

Was it you that thanked Him
For cloaking me in His love
Petitioning Him to look down below
From where He sits above?

And was it you that fasted
Cleansing in His name
Laying your all on the altar
Knowing each day He is the same?

Did you know He would answer?
Did you know He even heard?
When things moved not so quickly
You still rested in His word

I don't know just when you prayed
I only know the outcome
I rejoice and cry hallelujah
At where He's brought me from

Oh yes, I'm grateful for your life
And I want the whole world to see
I am who God says I am
Because you were praying for me

Songs of My People

A people without purpose
How far can they reach
A people without direction
How will they ever teach

A people without a voice
How will they speak their minds
A people without a vision
Inevitably remains blind

A people without hope
How can they go on
A people without great leaders
Remain divided and torn

A people without faith
To whom do they pray
A people without a Living God
Doomed to lose their way

A people with a stolen past
What songs will they sing?
They will sing songs of purpose
Until the bells of freedom truly ring

Precious Little Child

Precious little child
That I clothe and feed
I promise to fulfill
Above your basic needs

I promise to educate
By what I do and say
And to appreciate your existence
Each and every day

I will offer you comfort
When you feel alone or afraid
One of the many promises
Over time I have made

But above all else
I promise you my love
The only commitment greater
Comes from the Father above

Testimony

Lord, let my little light shine
Let it glow through the window and past the door
Let it shine to clothe the naked and feed the hungry
Comfort and embrace the poor

Let the words of my mouth
Bring a smile to someone's face
Let me take the time to say hello
And fellowship in your grace

Let my ten percent and offerings
Leave my pocket full of cheer
Expecting nothing in return
For my blessings are already here

Use my life as a testimony
Through my actions, words, and deeds,
For what good am I as a Christian
When I choose to ignore my brothers' need

Forgive me Lord for my second fruits
Be it my offering, talent or time
With everything that surround my senses
None can I claim as mine

Let my tears flow freely
As your spirit moves in me
Nothing like my soul opening up
When I put all my trust in thee

My prayers I offer up
My thanks I give to thee
Not because of favors I am asking
Just saying thanks for saving me

Whenever turmoil seeks me out
To the hills my eyes shall gaze
I will lift my hand and cry hallelujah in the midst of it
Glory to God is the highest praise!

Shedrick Jenkins

Shedrick Jenkins is an aspiring writer. He is from New York City and now resides in Columbia, SC. Through many trials and tribulations God has brought him through the fire. His goal is his testimony. His testimony is his story. God has opened his eyes to his gift so he's working toward writing his first manuscript.

Love Never Fails; God is Love

In this story, you will see how God has his hands in the mix. How he lets things happen for a reason. Also, how he makes a way out of things, because He wants to, if you believe.

This story starts out with this woman who always wanted to be an actress. She never got the right chance. She thought she did one day when she met this lawyer, but only to find out that he was in the black market business for new born babies. They both decided to make each other's dream come true.

The nightmare starts when she decides to change her mind about giving her baby up. The lawyer didn't want to hear any excuses. As this baby grew up, he became a man of God--doing things to please God. He married his high school sweet heart and had four kids, one girl and three boys. He was gifted and God blessed him. He was playing basketball in the NBA. One day, he lost it and got into drinking and drugs. Out of control he was about to lose everything. Then one night he cried out to God and found himself again.

That's why this story is called *Love Never Fails; God is Love,* because He is always there when we need him. Sometimes we just don't understand why He let things happen for the good or bad, but we do know it's for a reason.

He Kept Me

I use this title when I tell a little something about myself. If it was not for God's love, plan and protection for me, the life I used to live as leading me to perish at an early time in my life. So I give Him all the praise, honor and glory. I know that He is the source of my living.

I was born and raised in Brooklyn, NY by my mother and father. I had four sisters, and I was the only son. As I was growing up, my mother and father made sure my sisters and I had all we needed. I was pretty smart through out school. I didn't get into any serious trouble with the law as I saw other boys getting into trouble. We did have lots of rules to follow at home, but the biggest one was everybody goes to church on Sundays.

One of my dreams came true when I graduated from high school and went off to college to play basketball. My first year was good playing basketball and keeping my grades up. My second year, I was one of the star players heading toward good things. I couldn't handle the stardom though. Soon I lost it and became involved in sex, drugs, and rock & roll. It was those things that cost me my college and NBA career.

After my basketball career was over, I married my high school sweetheart and had four beautiful kids. I had one girl and three boys. After thirteen years of marriage, I lost it again, this time to drugs, strong music and the spoils of street life.

Now I am single and by myself. I have chosen God to lead and direct my life. I found out through out my years, that without God I am nothing, but with Him I can do all things. He is the source of my living. I can truly say that it was him that kept me all these years.

Love Never Fails; God is Love

(An Excerpt)

Pete walked into the club clean as a whistle with this dark blue pinstripe suit on. He is drawn to a pair of sexy red boots. As his wandering eyes travel up her coco brown toned legs, he makes eye contact with her. Her eyes were too beautiful; it sent chills down his spine.

At that moment he knew she was the one. As she was fumbling through her purse, Pete walked gracefully across the floor. By the time she found out what she was looking for, he was already behind her. With his smooth voice he whispered, "Can I buy you a drink?"

With a strange look on her face, she timidly accepts his offer. After talking, laughing and a few drinks, Pete says, "I could help you with your problem if you help me with mine."

Cathy Mitchem

Aspiring Christian novelist, beautician, Entrepreneur. Cathy is the proprietor of Cathy's Hair Styling Salon in Columbia, SC. Cathy began writing at an early age and is now desiring to pen her very first autobiography. God has given her many testimonies that has shaped her life as well as many others, but how many can benefit from it if they can not read about it. Look to the future for this author to be!

The Ice-Cream Man and the Corner Store

There was a family who lived in the 800 block of Park Street. This neighborhood was very poor. The children did not have toys to play with, so they played only with each other.

I was one of those children. While my mother would go to work, my oldest brother would keep us. Before she would leave for work, she would tell us not to leave the yard. One day we were playing on the porch and we heard the music from the Ice-cream truck. Everybody started running and yelling, “Ice-cream man, Ice-cream man! We took off running around the corner. We were running as fast as we could, but we lost him. We started going back home after we could not catch him.

My oldest brother was looking for us. We had forgotten what Mama told us. When he found us he said,

“I’m telling Mama, and she’s gonna get ya’ll.”

Although he had said that, he didn’t tell on us. By the time we had gotten home we saw all the other kids licking on their ice-cream smiling. We ask if we could get a lick off of their Popsicle.

The next Friday came and it was so hot. We decided to do the same thing again, but this time we got into trouble. On the way back, a pack of dogs started running after us. We ran and ran until we saw the corner store. The owner had the door open for us and let us in because he saw us crying. Our clothes were hanging off and we were out of breath. When we started looking around in the store, we saw candy, cookies, and ice cream.

The dog turned around because he was afraid of the man who owned the store. That was when we realized that this man's store was only two doors down from our house. It was closer, cheaper and cooler.

The corner represented Jesus Christ and the Ice-cream man represented the world We ran after things in the world until we couldn't run anymore. Psalms 46:1 states "God is our refuge and strength, a very present help in the time of trouble." Jesus' door is always open for us and he is always waiting for us to come in.